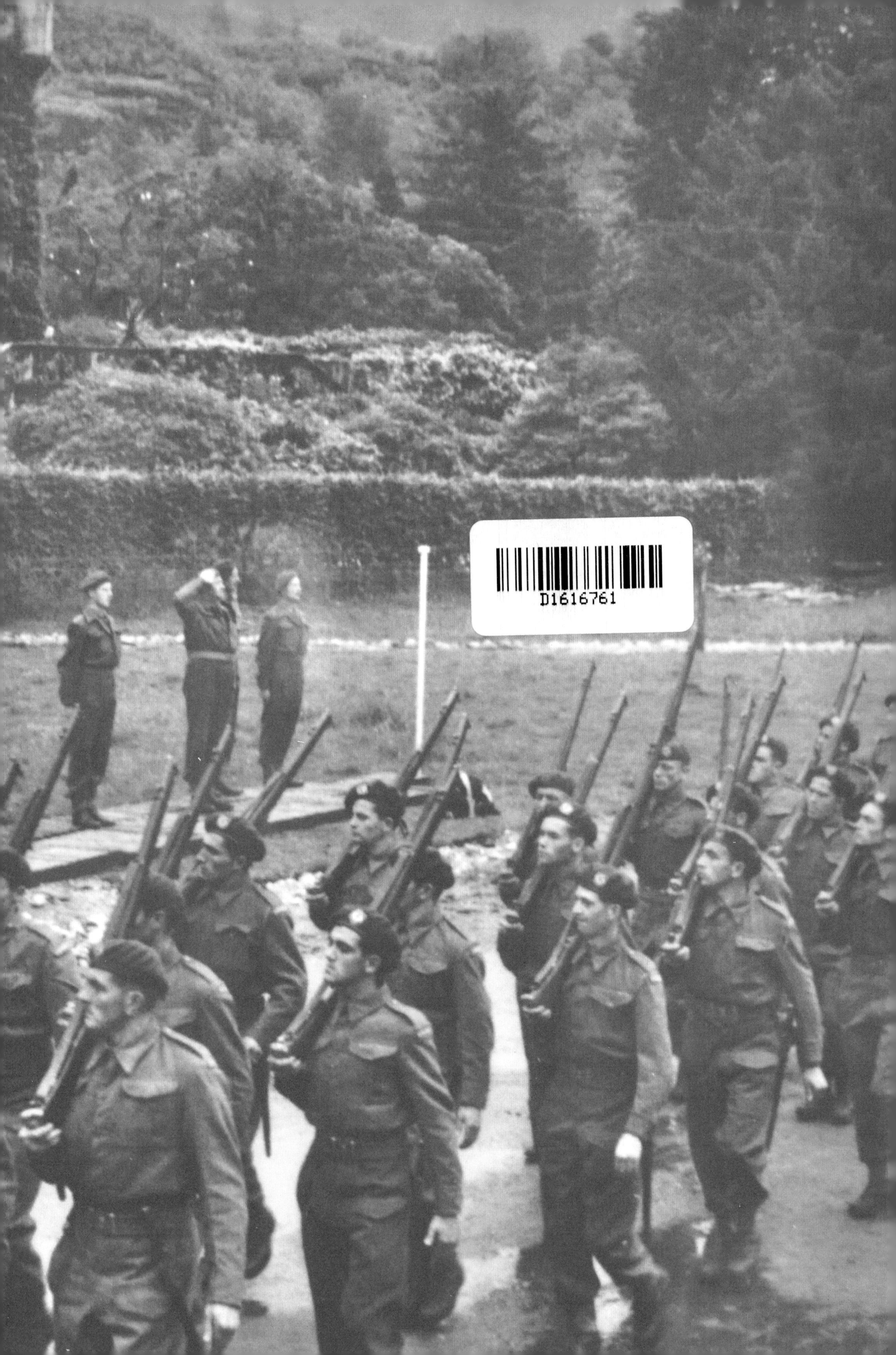

To Léon Gautier, who warmly welcomed me for the first time at Ouistreham in June 1994 and permitted me to meet his comrades from Kieffer Commando.

To Georges Fleury, another former Green Beret, who through his writings has perpetuated the memory of all Free French.

In memory of Joe Burnett, a British Commando, participant on the raid at Dieppe and of the Normandy landings in the vicinity of Ouistreham, died on 18 April 2009 at the age of 88 years.

To my father, an example of courage and of the spirit of resistance, with a passion for history, to whom I owe the discovery of the Kieffer Commando and who departed too early to see this book.

Cover Pages:

French Commandos marching out in front of Colonel Vaughan.
In the background is Achnacarry Castle, it accommodated the
Staffing-Committee and officers at the school.

June 6, very early in the afternoon. The Commandos progress
towards Saint-Aubin-d'Arquenay, the British lead and the
French come up from the rear.

 II

Preface By General Robert Bresse

Allied planning had foreseen a simultaneous assault on "Fortress Europe", with a double landing in the spring of 1944 in Normandy ("Overlord") and also in Provence ("Anvil Dragoon"). Not surprisingly, the French Army, now reconstituted in North Africa by merging the Free French Forces and the African Army, was destined for Provence.

The availability of maritime assets, however did not ultimately permit the simultaneity of these two operations. Priority was given to Normandy. For General de Gaulle the idea that the French might be absent on D-Day was intolerable. He insisted that the 2nd *Division Blindée* be channelled to England and integrated into operation "Overlord". Despite the effort, this great union was not going to happen on the primary echelons, for which the fighting forces had already been designated and the training had commenced. The French would not therefore be present in large numbers on D-Day, but they would be there in terms of quality. Four sticks, the precursors of the 2nd *Regiment de Chasseurs Parachutistes* (4th SAS) of the famous Special Air Service (SAS) Brigade, were parachuted into Brittany on the eve of the landings. The 1st *Battaillon de Fusiliers Marins Commandos* landed at Ouistreham at the head of Lord Lovat's equally famous 1st Special Service Brigade.

Philippe Kieffer's men had travelled a hard road for this. Although their chief had first conceived of the idea in March 1941, it was not until the end of April 1942 that the 1st *Compagnie de Fusiliers Marins* embarked on their ruthless Commando training. The unit was incorporated with the No.10 Inter-Allied Commando and was paraded in London on July 14 1942. It participated in operations on the coast of occupied Europe, expanding its manpower to become a battalion. In April 1944 it was integrated with the No.4 Franco-British Commando, formed with the Normandy landings in sight. The fighting spirit and effectiveness of these 177 French Commandos seduced Lord Lovat to the point of leading him to decide, very symbolically, that on D-Day they would be the first to set foot in France.

General Robert Bresse
Président de la Fondation de la France Libre

FONDATION DE LA FRANCE LIBRE

Table of Contents

III Preface by General Robert Bresse

p.2 1. Churchill remembers the Boer War

p.4 2. Norway stirs Philippe Kieffer into action

p.7 3. A training "enough to kill a horse" at Camp Achnacarry

p.16 4. From Dieppe to Scheveningen, the raids before D-Day

p.20 5. "Messieurs les Français, demain, les Boches, on les aura!"

p.28 6. A seaside resort transformed into a fortress

p.34 7. Dawson lets the french make the first landing

p.46 8. Commandos at Ouistreham try their luck at the casino

p.58 9. The weapons and equipment of the D-Day Commandos

p.62 10. From Ouistreham to Saint-Maclou, Three Months of Hard Fighting

p.68 11. From the landings in Holland to the birth of the Marine Commandos

p.70 12. Enemies of yesterday become friends at Ouistreham

p.72 11. Appendices 177 French Commandos on D-Day / The tale of the local photographer / The attack on the casino filmed at Port-en-Bessin

p.80 Sources & Websites / Photo Credits / With Thanks to / Places to visit

French Commandos sharpening their daggers in preparation for the landings. Faces on view from left to right are Andriot, Derrien and Lechaponnier. The last two would be wounded and evacuated on June 6.

Jean-Charles Stasi

KIEFFER
COMMANDO
THE FREE FRENCH
LANDINGS IN NORMANDY

Cover Drawing: Paul Gros

HEIMDAL

Churchill remembers the Boer War

Late spring 1940, Britain is practically disarmed after the evacuation of Dunkirk under German fire power, with only five hundred artillery pieces remaining available on its soil.

The British Prime Minister Winston Churchill had decided to create the Commandos in the late spring of 1940.

The British had lost 200 boats and 180 aeroplanes at Dunkirk, not to mention some 2,000 artillery pieces, 60,000 automotive vehicles, 76,000 tons of ammunition and 600,000 tons of carburant and supplies abandoned on the beaches.

Unable to launch a large-scale operation for which his country no longer had the means, Churchill therefore decided to hit "*Fortress Europe anywhere and at any time*" by targeted action assigned to troops, reduced in number, but still extremely determined. The idea had come to him from Lieutenant Colonel Dudley Clarke, an officer on the Staffing-Committee, on his return from Dunkirk.

The baptismal name of these new kinds of units came from the Prime Minister in person. From his time in the Boer War in South Africa, where he served as young officer at the beginning of the century, Churchill still had a vivid memory of the small groups of Afrikaner fighters called "commandos". Churchill, the Lieutenant and War Correspondent, returned home impressed with the audacity and effectiveness of these men, mostly farmers, vanishing into nature on foot or on horseback as soon as they had made their strike. And it did not escape him that their inferior number was largely compensated by the effect of surprise coupled with speed of action.

Formed from trained volunteers, many of whom had participated in the campaigns in France and Norway, the first Independent Companies became the Special

Service Battalion then the Special Service Brigade, and these were actually going to form the basis of the structure of the Commando organisation, whose numbers would continue to expand over the coming months. The first of these *"Mosquito bites"* to use Churchill's expression, were initiated on the night of June 23 to 24 1940, only two weeks after the retreat from Dunkirk. Operation "Collar" brought together one hundred and twenty men, for the most part volunteers from the Territorial Army.

Between the 27 May and 4 June 1940, Operation "Dynamo" permitted the evacuation of nearly 350,000 men out of the Dunkirk pocket.

Their goal : to disrupt and push back German defences to a zone located between Boulogne and Le Touquet, but because of inadequate preparation and a glaring lack of appropriate equipment, the raid was not a success. This did not prevent the population from welcoming back the Commandos as heroes at Dover.

The second operation (code named "Ambassador") just one month later, had targeted Guernsey in the Channel Islands. This was a disaster. At the time of re-embarking, a ship sunk, a man drowned and three others who could not swim had to be abandoned on the spot where they were quickly captured.

On hearing the account of this fiasco, Churchill thundered out his orders *"that there should never again be a "Guernsey"!"* So in the wake of this, Combined Operations were created, specially dedicated to these special missions.

Under the direction of Admiral Sir Roger Keyes, the last months of 1940 were punctuated with raids destined to *"Set Europe on fire,"* in Winston Churchill's own words. At the beginning of 1941 the escalation in power of this new weapon was palpable. On March 4, the raid against the port facilities on the Lofoten Islands, off Narvik, resulted in the destruction of twenty plants and eleven ships weighing almost eighteen thousand tons. Nearly four million litres of oil and carburant went up in smoke. Over two hundred Germans and a good sixty Norwegian collaborator employees were taken back to Britain.

In addition, the British had shipped out some three hundred young Norwegians, mostly sailors, eager to go to England to enlist in the Free Norwegian Forces. The success of operation "Claymore" had a strong impact throughout the whole of the United Kingdom, which was suffering murderous attacks of the *Luftwaffe* on an almost daily basis. In towns and villages, newspapers could be had, devoting whole front pages to the exploits of these men with blackened faces, transported on weird barges from the distant coasts of Norway and who then, in a very short time, had sewn the seeds of the death and destruction to the enemy. At Lofoten, these Commandos, of which the British population had only just discovered their existence, applied the full force of their fighting spirit and initiative. Through their efficiency in close hand to hand combat and the action of urban guerrilla warfare, they proved that the tactics of war would be changed forever.

Exhausted by the retreat and the recent fighting, some British soldiers are piled onto the deck of a boat. In a few hours they will depart for England.

Norway stirs Philippe Kieffer into action

Spurred on by the success of the raid on the Lofoten Islands in March 1941, Philippe Kieffer ended up convincing the British to accept French soldiers into the ranks of the Commandos. A great adventure was about to begin.

One morning in early March 1941, groups of intrigued Londoners could be seen crowding around newspaper stands. One man who had just come off the Portsmouth train steered himself towards a little group forming at the exit of the station. He was slightly balding, big and broad built. His clear eyes were calmly assured, in keeping with his imposing figure. He too wanted to find out what had stirred such enthusiasm among the locals even though they had just been shaken by a new air alert, a lengthy alert causing a major delay to his train journey.

His name was Philippe Kieffer, he was 42 years old and of French Alsatian origin. Born in Haiti on October 24, 1899, he had pursued graduate studies in Commerce in the United States. During the thirties, he had been Co-Director of the National Bank of the Republic of Haiti and Secretary of the Chamber of Commerce in Haiti. At the outbreak of war he became Policy Advisor to the National City Bank in London. Recalled in September 1939 to the forces on the ground as a Sub-Lieutenant, he was transferred one month later to the Navy as a Quartermaster second-class, assigned to the Staffing-Committee of Admiral Abrial, Commander of the Theatre of Operations in the North. In the spring of 1940, Kieffer had lived through the site of the disaster at Dunkirk and the incredible evacuation of the British Expeditionary Force. A fortnight after Operation "Dynamo", he had secured a voyage to England on board a trawler *Le Tonneau* leaving Saint-Vaast-la-Hougue, in the Channel.

The first French officers who responded to General de Gaulle's sounding were presented to Winston Churchill. Philippe Kieffer stands second from the left.

By March 4, 1941, the British Commandos were preparing to land on the Lofoten Islands in Norway.

The raid on the Lofoten Isles had destroyed twenty factories and eleven ships of nearly eighteen thousand tons.

Upon his arrival on British soil, he was assigned to the old cruiser Courbet anchored just off Portsmouth Harbour, to the anti-aircraft battery and floating barracks of the Free French Naval Forces (FNFL); then promoted to Second-Maître in July 1940 then to *officier de réserve* "interpreting and figures", in october of the same year. Yet Philippe Kieffer had only one thought in mind: to resume the struggle against the Germans. So it was with great relish that he devoured, in his turn, the headlines on the daily newspapers: "BRITISH TROOPS RAID THE LOFOTEN ISLES"splashed across the front page of the daily he had just bought. After reading the article, he understood the full measure of the impact of this news on English morale.

"All the objectives attached to the operation were met with complete success. Nine German merchant ships and a Norwegian boat under German control were sunk along with an armed Merchant Navy vessel", as the paper relayed according to the official statement, adding *"our troops had met little opposition."*

The success of the raid reinforced his determination as to, *"Why a group of Frenchmen, himself included, should not have the same right to go with their British comrades, risking their lives, even for a few hours, on a corner of the coast of France. (...) The faster the better because a soldier carrying weapons would also bring courage and hope to the French Resistance. How to better serve at this moment?"* he asked himself. [1] Armed with this fighting spirit, which was one of the hallmark traits of his personality, Kieffer spoke persuasively about it to Vice-Admiral Muselier, Commander of the Free France Naval Forces, so much so that the British authorities would end up accepting the principle of having the French integrated into the Commandos. Kieffer would later learn that the decisive argument was not his promises of unwavering commitment and foolproof fighting, but more prosaically, the offer of the recruits, who knew better than anyone else the French coast from Dunkirk to Bayonne.

The first sixteen candidates of the Green Berets were placed under the orders of Premier Maître Vourch Francis, who had left Cherbourg on board a high-speed launch on 19 June 1940. These men, eager for battle against the Germans, came from all backgrounds and the most diverse environments; Wandelaer was an ex-legionnaire, Jean, a French national who had immigrated to Brazil and had been burning to return to the homeland and dreamt of rediscovering the capital. Corsica Loverini was already a marksman of formidable accuracy. The there was Tanniou, a lanky and taciturn Breton; Simon with shoulders like a colossus and the split nostrils of a boxer, then Errard, nicknamed "Bombshell Skull", Baloche, the smallest of the band at only five foot and two and a half inches, and there was Briat, who had been a young officer on the vessel *Île de France* when war was declared. Added to this were a handful of hotheads punished for breaches of discipline or brawls after drinking. This embryonic French unit underwent its first training sessions at the instruction camp at Camberley starting in mid-January 1942. At this point the fighting force was joined by Jean Pinelli, a teacher of physical education in civilian life and who over the coming weeks would prove an instructor of the first order. In early March, they were transferred to the Royal Marines at Eastney, near Portsmouth for a three-week course devoted to handling light weapons. At the end of this training, the thirty men still in the running took to the road to the British Navy shore establishment HMS Royal Arthur at Skegness, two hundred kilometers north of London. In January 1942, the rave ratings issued by their instructors finally opened the doors to the "*creme de la creme*" of the British armed forces: the Commando Basic Training Centre at Achnacarry in Scotland. They were expected in late April, and only those who emerged successfully would be able to wear the Green Beret and to be called "Commando".

Kieffer recruits in training during the summer of 1942, led by John Pinelli, professor of physical education in the civilian sector; note that future Commandos still wear the French Caps or the "bachi", the French Naval beret.

The training of the first French candidates for the Green Berets; as seen in this photo, some of Philippe Kieffer's recruits are still wearing the regulation French army helmet.

(1) Unless otherwise indicated, all information regarding Philippe Kieffer reported in this book are excerpts from his memoirs, *Béret Vert*, éditions France-Empire.

A training "enough to kill a horse" at Achnacarry

The obligatory destination for obtaining the famous Green Beret was the school for Commandos at Achnacarry, lost in the mountains of Scotland. In some ways, a hell before paradise for the French volunteers led by Philippe Kieffer.

In some ways, one could say that Lieutenant-Colonel Vaughan had a sense of humour. At the entrance of the Commando Basic Training Centre that he had been given the honour to command, he built a fake cemetery over which the newcomers had to march. The causes of death of the 'trainees' here were very legibly displayed on the crosses of the eighteen fictitious graves. Apparently, one of them had had a fatal fall on account of being poorly fastened during the abseiling session, another had raised his head too high as he crawled beneath live rounds of machine gun fire, a third did not observe a sufficiently safe distance during the use of explosives...

In short, even before they had crossed the threshold, each candidate in the berets had had experience of what was in store. In fact, a foretaste had come even earlier right at the moment they arrived at Spean Bridge (a simple platform without a station), which

Lieutenant-Colonel Charles Vaughan

As Kieffer's men quickly realised, Lieutenant-Colonel Vaughan (1899-1974) was not a tender man. This former Chief Warrant Officer of the Coldstream Guards, one of the oldest regiments in the guard, joined the Commandos at their inception and participated in the very first raids in the summer of 1940.

During the operation on the Lofoten Islands in March 1941, he was marked out by his superiors for *"his energy, his spirit of initiative and his leadership over the men"*, without forgetting *"his determination to obtain from his men exactly what he wanted to achieve."* Qualities that led general Dudley Clarke, founder of the Commandos, to choose him to direct the Commando Basic Training Centre as soon as it opened and to establish the course content which was a justifiably harsh content, just like its designer.

was the nearest stop to Sir Donald Cameron of Locheil's Castle in Achnacarry at the foot of Ben Nevis, the highest mountain in the British Isles. This domain of several thousand hectares of woods, mountains and lakes, owned by one of the oldest and most illustrious clans in Scottish nobility, had now been requisitioned by the British army staff to form, under the worst possible conditions, its elite fighters.

Trainees were housed in these buildings shaped like half-barrels, the Nissen huts, which also housed canteens and washroom facilities.

At the entrance of the camp, these fictitious graves were there to remind newcomers of the dangers of training and to encourage them to observe safety instructions.

Coming off the train on April 28 1942, in the late afternoon, hungry and tired from their long journey, the small group of thirty Free Frenchmen were relieved to see the trucks that were supposed to take them to their final destination. They were quickly disillusioned. With just a hint of irony, Charles Vaughan informed Kieffer and his men that they only had the right to deposit their bags in these, and that they would have to transport themselves through twenty five miles of Highlands separating them from the camp, on foot.

On approaching their destination some lively Scottish music helped them forget their fatigue and reminded the members of the *1ère Compagnie de fusiliers marins* (1st Company of Naval Rifles) that they were the first foreign volunteers to enter into the holy of holies of the British armed forces.

"Here's what happens to those who don't follow instructions carefully and do what they should not do ..." was their welcoming speech, and the fictitious graves were pointed out to the newcomers also reminding them that from each squad of forty men coming through the camp, there would be an average of one death and two or three wounded.

From the very first day, the French would be subjected to a physical regime that would *"kill a horse"*, as Kieffer later recalled in his memoirs. For starters, walking was prohibited. From sunrise to sunset, one needed to move in quick step under the wing of commanding officers who would not stop yelling with machine gun force. As soon as the porridge oats were swallowed the Green Beret candidates were subjected to treatment that would make all their past endurance pale in comparison.

Everything was done to repel them, to eliminate the weak ones, especially the less determined. It was necessary to leap up without flinching when the duty sergeant burst into the corrugated iron hut shaped like a half-barrel, where apprentice Commandos had just fallen asleep after a more strenuous day than the last: *"Rally in ten minutes, full campaign dress, marching at night with full equipment!"*...and pressing on thirty kilometers to the compass through a desolate landscape, their faces protected from the icy wind by a "Cap-comfort", a band of khaki wool used interchangeably as hat, scarf, or even a cagoule.

The next day, waking up after only two or three hours of sleep, they underwent the daily inspection on the Parade Ground, clean-shaven, impeccably dressed in battle gear and shoes as bright on the bottom as on the top.

Strength exercises were carried out with telegraph poles or tree trunks.

The techniques of unarmed combat, highly prized by Commandos, were perfected by Captain WE Fairbairn, who was inspired by the martial arts he had been able to study while serving in the Shanghai Police Force.

Between the close-combat, the "obstacle course", the barehanded sessions, abseiling, the boxing, shooting with all types of weapons, physical education and explosive handling sessions, the new recruits did not have a minute to themselves. In the evening, they were so exhausted that they could not even think about having a pint at the bar. They knew that their nights were short and would bring lots of new suffering.

Trainees placed in conditions as close as possible to real combat.

A disarmed Commando needed to know how to face an enemy threatening him with a rifle equipped with a bayonet.

Lieutenant Charles Trepel in full demonstration mode for handling a fighting knife, the Commandos' symbolic weapon.

Introduction for the handling of the toggle rope, a rope of about 1 meter 50 supplied to each Commando that could be tied together for obstacle clearance. Joined end to end, several toggled ropes enable the rapid forging of a "V" or monkey bridge.

Both men in full swing wearing the "Cap comfort" on their heads, a woollen khaki band that the Commandos used interchangeably as hat, scarf, or even cagoule.

Move quickly, whatever the obstacles! One of the basics of Commando training.

Scaling exercises, with the help of a rope or their bare hands, were common because they reinforced stamina and helped overcome vertigo.

The trainees conduct landing exercises on Spean Lake near Achnacarry, most often under real mortar or machine gun fire.

The Commando candidates also successively trained in residential areas.

One of the most feared events was the famous "seven miles", which was run in less than sixty minutes while carrying individual weapons and a backpack that could weigh up to forty kilos.

At the first failure the French intern was labelled "froggy". The second failure was sanctioned by a judgment without appeal, the: Return to unit. In other words, back to square one and goodbye for good to the prestigious Green Berets.

More speed marches were incorporated into the program of festivities: 12 miles in less than two and a half hours and about 20 miles in less than five hours. It was during the course of those endless speed marches that the spirit of the Commandos was truly fashioned. Indeed, there would always come a time when one of the men suffered sudden fatigue or discouragement. If he was well integrated with the rest of the group, he knew he would find comrades to carry his bag and his weapon. Otherwise, he would leave them at the roadside and then it only remained for him to take the train and quit the camp for the last time.

Another formidable test was to jump head first from a truck travelling around twenty-five miles per hour. If the movement was executed correctly, it redressed the candidate's momentum and all ended well. But woe to those who did not make a clean dive, usually, he would not be able to get himself up unaided from the roadside.

Crossing with a monkey bridge, formed with toggle-ropes under mortar fire, to acclimatise the rooky Commandos to war conditions.

Learning how to cross barbed wire, with or without a gun, would prove very useful to Kieffer's men as to other Commandos.

12

Future Commandos also encountered landing exercises on Spean Lake near Achnacarry. They needed to reach the shore from rowing boats or small barges, often under a barrage of live machine gun fire, grenades and mortars.

And woe to those who forgot safety instructions! Being hit by a burst of fire or an explosive could unwittingly contribute to extending the alignment of graves at the entrance to the camp...

Over the weeks, the French witnessed the transformation of their bodies at the same time as they felt their mentality harden along with the muscles in their chest, in their arms and their legs.

"*Anyone can become Commando, provided you have the strength and in particular, the willpower to bear the terrible training on a daily basis*", repeated the chief instructor as the leitmotif.

Kieffer, who could have been the father of most of the guys under his command, endured just as much of this inhuman regime. He knew he needed to set an example if he wanted to be a respected leader in combat. Anyway, he had no choice at Achnacarry; there was no difference between the program for officers and men.

Some nights when no night exercise was scheduled, the recruits were entitled to conferences or screenings of the raids accomplished by Commandos in occupied Europe, and also in Crete and Libya. In each case, the speaker was a teacher who had himself participated in the operation in question and who knew, using his passionate tone and the details of the story, how to inspire an already conquered audience.

It was during one of these meetings that Kieffer's men heard of the denouement of the incredible

Although the landing craft would be larger, come D-Day, Kieffer's men would remember their landing exercises on the Scottish lakes, and the live ammunition!

raid on Saint-Nazaire, during Operation "Chariot". On the night of March 27 to 28 of the same year, 1942, Lord Mountbatten, Commander in Chief of Combined Operations, sent an old American destroyer the *Campbeltown*, disguised as a *Kriegsmarine* ship, toward the watertight doors of the gigantic Joubert lock, the only dry dock on the entire Atlantic coast large enough to accommodate the great German battleship Tirpitz, sister ship of the Bismarck which was sunk by the Royal Navy at the end of the epic battle on May 27, 1941.

The Commandos on board the *Campbeltown* and those transported by the fifteen escort vessels had, in just a few hours, inflicted heavy losses on the enemy coastal defences such as the port facilities. As if this was not enough to plunge the German garrison into panic, late morning, the explosion of the destroyer packed with delayed-charges reduced to a pulp all the German military, of

Two years later, came the great leap forward onto the beaches at Normandy...

which many officers had boarded the wreck already littered with corpses.

Certainly, the human toll had also been heavy on the British side, with 169 dead and 215 prisoners out of little more than 600 men. But the audacity of the raid, described by some of the participants as a suicide mission, had strengthened the resolve of the British and given a little hope to occupied Europe at the same time as throwing Hitler into a rage. This latter does not explain how the attackers, with this "old tub", this "shell of a vessel" had been able to reach Saint-Nazaire without being detected and neutralised, the Loire estuary was regarded by the Germans as the best defended on the Atlantic coastal area. In short, as summarised by Kieffer, these raids *reinforced our commitment to forging new exploits that could be added to the long list of this glorious elite army.*

After ten weeks of training, the French company left Achnacarry with outstanding marks. Only one of its members had been rejected. All the others had earned the title of Commando.

At the beginning of the summer of 1942, the 1st *Compagnie de Fusiliers Marins* became 1 Troop of allied No.10 Commando, newly created by the British authorities to cope with the massive influx of foreign volunteers. Besides the French, this unit would host Belgians, Poles, Norwegians, and also Germans who were opposed to Nazism.

On 14 July 1942, Kieffer and his men, along with the other components of the Free French, had the honour of marching in London, where they were paraded before General de Gaulle. Numerous people came along to see for themselves these "fighting French Commandos" that the press had paid tribute to with headlines and pictures on the front page. *"The most celebrated of the parade were the French Commandos, newly created, ruddy faced men tanned by the training on British beaches"* recounted one of the dailies.

In the weeks and months that followed, the French Commandos would have more than one opportunity to show their fighting spirit and increase their popularity among the British.

A precious document: the only known photo of one of the two French Troops who landed at Normandy. This is 8 Troop, photographed on 14 July 1943, at Camp Achnacarry. Maurice Chauvet, one of Kieffer's men, took this picture together with the numbers and names of his comrades.

1er B.F.M.C. _ 1o IA. COMMANDO _ TROOP 8 _ 14. JULY. 1943

A _ Cap. de JONGH   B _   C _ Cap. TREPEL   D _ Cap. D.H. BURR

1. NEVEN	13. GANNAT	25. PAILLET	37. FREJAVISE	49. GROSSI	61. ERNAULT
2. CAUSSE	14. GUILCHER	26. LAOT	38. LETANG	50. GAUTIER	62. ARCHERI
3. BOLZER	15. FOURER	27. NAUD	39. CHAUSSE	51. BOULANGER	63. AGNERRE
4. BASCOULERGUE	16. COPPIN	28. MESSANOT	40. LE GALL	52. PAOLI	64. JUNG
5. PREVOST	17. FOUGERE	29. CABANELLA	41. HORNY	53. RIVEAU	65. CEVOS-MAMI
6. CAILLE	18. PINEL	30. ALLAIN	42. SCHERER	54. FOLLIOT	66. DEVILLERS
7. TROYARD	19. BRIAND. J	31. GUY	43. KLOPFEINSTEIN	55. LE RESTE	67. CHAUVET
8. BALLARO	20. GALTON	32. HOURCOURIGARAY	44. LT HULOT	56. DUCASSE	68. CHAPELAIN
9. GACHARD	21. STRINA	33. GUIMBAULT	45. LT LOFI	57. MARIACCIA	69. CROIZER
10. MAILLET	22. MASSIN	34. ROUGIER	46. LAVEZZI	58. LOGEAIS	70. PLANCHER
11. RIVIERE	23. LE RIGOLEUR	35. LE HALPER	47. VINAT	59. BRIAND. G	
12. ROUELANDT	24. LE CHAPONIER	36. GUILLOU	48. LESCA	60. LE GAC	

From Dieppe to Scheveningen, the raids before D-Day

The raid on Dieppe in August 19, 1942 marked the beginning of operational activities for the French Commandos. They were repeated many times, sometimes tragically, before the landings on 6 June 1944.

Kieffer's men, now freshly bereted, continued training in Wales among the No.10 Inter-Allied Commando, while the largest operation on the French coasts since the beginning of the war was looming - Code Name: "Jubilee". This time with reduced staffing, it acted more as a helping hand, just like during the very first raids of 1940. Prefiguring what would become Operation "Overlord", some six thousand men, five thousand of which were Canadians, needed to land on the beaches of Dieppe with the reinforcement of assault tanks. The Allies wanted to show the Germans that they could now expect combined large-scale action, everywhere and at any time. This would thereby bring Hitler to strengthen his defences on the Atlantic coast, in response to repeated requests from Stalin to open a second front in the west to relieve pressure in the East. Fifteen French Commandos were selected to be part of the first assault troops. The officier des équipage (Crews-Officer) Francis Vourch and six men (Dumenoir, Simon, Jean, Loverini, Borretini and Tanniou) were integrated into a Canadian unit before landing in Dieppe itself. Moutailler, de Wandelaer, Errard, Caesar and Roppert joined the No.3 British Commando who needed to intervene in the Berneval sector. As for Baloche, Taverne and Rabouhans they were integrated into Lord Lovat's No.4 Commandos.

"Jubilee" would be a bloody failure. Of the six thousand men landed, there were some three thousand five hundred killed, wounded and imprisoned. Twenty-eight Churchill tanks had to be abandoned on the shingle strewn shore along with corpses and destroyed barges. Two of the fifteen French Commandos were missing. *Second Maître* Moutailler considered by Kieffer as one of his best men was killed, presumably finished off by the Germans as he lay seriously injured on the beach. As for the quartermaster Caesar,

former legionnaire, he was taken prisoner in the late morning. Transferred to a train for Germany, he managed to jump from the freight car while the train was travelling at low speed. After an eventful journey during which he was arrested again, Caesar eventually arrived back in England via Gibraltar on June 6, 1943.

Second Maître Raymond Wandelaer, recognisable by his French petty-officer cap, along with British soldiers of No.3 Commando, with whom he participated in the raid on Dieppe.

On the right sleeve of Raymond Wandelaer, we can see very clearly the insignia worn by French Commandos in 1942: a "banana" - "France", a title "Commando" and the flag of the Beaupré Cross of Lorraine.

A month later on July 14, the same Caesar was decorated in London for his actions at Dieppe, along with four comrades who also participated in "Jubilee": Ropert, Taverne, Rabouhans and Baloche. Second Maître Baloche was particularly honoured as the first French Commando to receive the Military Medal. Furthermore, this was from the hand of Lord Mountbatten himself, chief of Combined Operations. The little Norman owed this high distinction to his efficiency with knives against the battery artillery operators at Varengeville.

In just one year, the number of French Commandos had expanded and the 1st *Compagnie de Fusiliers Marins* gave way to the 1st *Battaillon de Fusiliers Marins Commandos* (*BFMC*). At the end of August 1942, the newly bereted candidates were thus passed to 1 Troop, made up of fifty to eighty-one men. They came from France, North Africa and Spain as in the case of Maurice Chauvet and Pierre-Charles Boccadoro, who had spent long months in prisons and camps under Franco. In early autumn 1942, while they were still stationed at Criccieth in Wales, No.1 Troop was now complete. Lieutenant Trépel took command of the 1st section and *sous-lieutenant* Guy Vourch the 2nd Section. The reinforcement of forty-five additional recruits from Lebanon, led by Crew-Lieutenant Alexander Lofi, had created a second Troop, 8 Troop, in the spring of 1943. Many of these men had joined the Free French in 1940 and among them there were a large number of Bretons. This was the case for the Rennais (a native of Rennes) Léon Gautier, who was carrying out his naval Gunner training on the *Courbet* when a resounding call from a certain General de Gaulle came over the BBC radio air waves. He had embarked as a gunner on the old freighter Gallois, ploughing between Scotland and Newfoundland to load iron ore, he had a brief stint on the submarine *Surcouf*, before joining the unit of French marines fusiliers bound for Beirut. A few months later, when they gave him a choice between joining the army in North Africa, commanded by General Giraud, or returning to England to enlarge the ranks of the Commandos, he did not hesitate much. Eager for battle as soon as possible against the Germans, the young Breton with the solid character had also been attracted by the elite soldiers whose reputation was growing fast.

In addition to this extra Troop, the 1st *Bataillon de fusiliers marins Commandos* (*BFMC*) were furnished with a K Gun section (rapid fire machine-gun) containing twenty three men under the command of Peter Amaury, a young lieutenant from the Army.

From autumn 1943, thirty French Commandos would participate in raids in occupied territory, operating on some occasions beside the British Green Berets.

With Philippe Kieffer at their head, French Commandos parade in London on 14 July 1943, on the occasion of their National Day. Just as in the previous year, they are warmly cheered and applauded by the population.

The insignia worn by French Commandos on their right shoulder during the raid on Dieppe on 19 August 1942.

These operations were of the utmost importance for the preparation of the Allied landings in Europe, the principle of which has been decided by Churchill and Roosevelt at the Tehran conference (28 November - 1 December). These sounding operations on the coast

London, July 14 1943. For bravery at Dieppe, Second Maître Baloche (foreground) was awarded the Military Medal. Like his fellow soldiers in the 1st *BFMC*, Baloche wears on his green beret the Beaupré Cross of Lorraine flag, symbol of Free France.

Maître Wallerand, who here leads 1 Troop at the parade on July 14 1943 in London, was killed five months later, on the night of December 24 to 25, during the raid on Gravelines.

Le pavillon de Beaupré à croix de Lorraine, emblème de la France libre.

unearth mines to refer to specialists who were working on D-Day preparations, to photograph German defences at low tide, to cut a fragment of the metal barriers that Rommel had crammed along the beaches to shred the landing craft. At the head of a squad of eight men, Lieutenant Vourch reported to Quinéville on the Cotentin peninsula, to survey a German minefield, samples of sand and gravel, as well as sketches of bunkers protecting that part of shore. This precious "harvest" brought Francis Vourch the Military Cross, the third highest British military decoration.

Not all the French Green Berets would return from these particularly risky raids. On Christmas Eve 1943, the officier de l'équipages Wallerand drowned, frozen stiff and exhausted, while trying to swim towards the high-speed launch that was stationed just off the beach at Gravelines. Once his mission was accomplished, he was unable to use his dinghy as it was filled with water. He went down, just ten meters from the Royal Navy boat that was trying to recuperate him. The other five members of his Commando (Caron, Meunier, Navrault, Pourcelot and Madec) managed to get away from the Germans and at the same time escape certain death. After many adventures, they all managed to return to England and reintegrate into the Commandos.

For the French, the most tragic raid would be one on 27 February 1944 on the beach at Scheveningen, Holland. Directed by Captain Trepel, a small group needed to gather information on the exact location of a factory specialising in the manufacture of the new German secret weapon, which later proved to be the V1 flying bomb and its successor the V2. Worried about not seeing the return of the Commandos, the commander of the speedboat gave the order to haul in the rope connecting his boat to the dory which had permitted them to reach the shore. The line was cut and they would never again see Captain Trepel and his five comrades: Jean Hagneré, Roger Cabanella, Fernand Devillers, René Guy and Jacquelin River. The disappearance of Charles Trepel was a huge blow to Kieffer, who considered him a *"personal friend and officer of great value"*, but also for all the men of the 1st *BFMC* who were attached to this exemplary officer for his skill and courage, just as hard on his subordinates as on himself. The bodies of the six men would be found during the liberation

of France, the Netherlands or the Channel Islands all had the same goal: to report back maximum information about the German defences that punctuated the Atlantic Wall.

Small groups of men with blackened faces were transported at night by submarine or rapid speed launch. Approaching the coast, they were put into the water in their dry suits, or embarked on inflatable life rafts to start paddling, taking care not to cause any waves. Within a handful of hours, they needed to take samples of sand to determine if a tank was likely to get stuck on this part of the shore, to detect and of Holland, summarily buried under false identities as "RAF airmen". The tragic operation at Scheveningen would be the last entrusted to the French Commandos before June 6, 1944. One month later, the order arrived to abort all prepared raids. In mid April, the 1st *BFMC* was integrated into the No.4 British Commando, commanded by the young Colonel Dawson, who had been brought up in Lausanne and spoke perfect French, tinged with a vaudois accent (from the

Transported by high-speed launches, Commandos with blackened faces slip onto the beaches to gather valuable information at the peril of their lives.

The Commandos return from Dieppe, with face markings. We can see to the right a dories, the light landing craft used by the Green Berets during their nocturnal raids on the coasts of France and Holland.

Swiss Vaud region). The "4" became the first and only Franco-British Commando. It was composed of three French Troops and four British Troops, each fortified by five to six officers and about seventy men. If one added the Command Post and communications/transmissions sections, this made a total of about six hundred officers, NCOs/second-officers and soldiers.

No.4 Commando was transferred to the pretty seaside resort of Bexhill on the opposite coast to the Pas-de-Calais in France. The whole of the south of England was now nothing more than an enormous military camp bulging with men and equipment.

Undoubtedly, the large-scale landing on the French coast was coming soon, and Kieffer's men, pumped up and sharp as the blades of their daggers, were eager to play their part.

Captain Charles Trépel

The first official French Commando, Charles Trepel was born in 1908 in Odessa. His family left Russia for Germany at the time of the Bolshevik Revolution. The rise of Nazism pushed the young Trepel to leave for France. Called up in September 1939 in France, he was demobilised after the armistice of 1940 with the rank of lieutenant. Wanting to continue the fight, he managed to get to England via Gibraltar and enlisted in the Free French Forces.

In spring 1942, he became Kieffer's second at the head of the French Commandos then in the course of being established. A year later, he was elevated to the rank of Captain and took command of 8 Troop which had just been created. With an unusual strength of character which was just as hard on himself as on his men, Charles Trepel was the archetypal Commando leader capable of completing two "speed marches" of 10 miles each fully loaded with weapons and equipment. As well as being his friend, his death in Holland in February 1944 deprived Philippe Kieffer of a valuable right hand man.

Since 1947, a Marine Commando has borne his name. Based in Lorient, it has been attached to the Special Operations Command since 1992.

"Messieurs les Français, demain, les Boches, on les aura!"

Transported to a huge camp near Southampton, without any contact with the outside world, Kieffer's men understood that the day they had been waiting for so long was now very close.

For those, like Maurice Chauvet, who had experienced internment in France or Spain before gaining passage to England, the camp at Tichfield brought back bad memories. Located near Southampton, this immense enclosure was surrounded by barbed wire and guarded by American soldiers who were ordered to shoot on sight the slightest attempt to leave. In

addition, a no-man's land stood between the camp and the first habitation. However, this impression was quickly dispelled. Upon arrival in late May 1944, the men in No.4 Franco-British Commando realised that their stay - the length of which they did not know – could turn out to be rather agreeable. Totally incommunicado, released from chores via an auxiliary battalion, the Commandos had nothing else to do but perfect their physical condition and prepare for their mission. They were also able to watch westerns in the big tent, converted into a cinema or enjoy the bright sunshine and spring temperatures that had prevailed on the Channel coasts since the beginning of the month. Loudspeakers broadcast country or jazz music all day long. This little corner of America was reinforced by Coca-Cola served without restriction. At dinner time, the French also discovered self-service where one ate the contents of ones tray while still advancing in an interminably long queue.

The Combined Operations badge, worn on the shoulder by all British Commandos.

The insignia of the 1st Battalion de fusiliers marins commandos, created by Maurice Chauvet in early 1944. On it is represented a shield of the brig Adventure transversed by the Commando dagger. A cross of Lorraine is contained on the canton dexter of the shield.

The "banana" carried on the shoulder of the men of No.4 Franco-British Commando.

For disembarkation, No.4 Commando was integrated with the 1st Special Service Brigade (1st Commando Brigade), which also included Commandos 3 and 6, along with the 45th Royal Marine Commando. The 1st Special Service Brigade was commanded by Lord Lovat, a descendent of ancient Scottish nobility, Peer of the House of Lords. A veteran of the raids on Norway and Dieppe, this officer of 33 years of age with his

1st Special Service Brigade

Formed for the invasion of Normandy, this unit included men from No.3, 4 and 6 Commandos and the 45th Royal Marine Commando, with a total of about three thousand men. Its leader, Lord Lovat was 33 years old in 1944, from old Scottish nobility; he was one of the first volunteers to join the Commandos in July 1940. With a charismatic personality, Lord Lovat inspired confidence in his men. This man was an original; he would land on June 6, armed with a hunting rifle, wearing khaki corduroy pants, a white turtleneck sweater and a suede vest without sleeves: *"To each his Boche. You are going to show us what you can do..."* He declared to Kieffer's men on the eve of D-Day.

N°4 Commando

Formed in Ayr (Scotland) in July 1940, it was one of the most glorious of the British Commandos. This was illustrated by the raids in Norway, Boulogne and Dieppe, where it was the only one to have much success in those days. Brigadier General Lord Lovat, who was in command from the outset, had passed the torch to young Lieutenant-Colonel Robert Dawson in order to devote himself to the formation of the 1st Special Service Brigade.

Born into a military family, Robert Dawson was educated in Switzerland, where he acquired his mastery of French. Despite his young age he was already an officer of superior experience, a veteran of the operations at Lofoten and Dieppe.
After the operations in Normandy, No.4 Commando would be engaged in Holland in late 1944.

In this photo, a few weeks before the landings, French officers surround Colonel Dawson, commander of No.4 Commando.

long silhouette and fine moustache, was held in high esteem by the French Commandos, who by now had had their beret badge redesigned by Maurice Chauvet as the flag of Beaupré, the cross of Lorraine. A seasoned war chief, Brigadier General Lovat could appreciate their fighting at Dieppe and knew the courage and efficiency that they had displayed during the raids that followed. He announced to Kieffer that he and his men would have the honour of being the first to set foot in France.

Using photos and relief maps where all the locations indicated were replaced by code names, the Commandos familiarised themselves with their landing zone. This is when they discovered that their primary objective was to storm a small coastal town, to seize the port and to safeguard intact the lock at the mouth of a canal. To achieve this, they would need to reduce to silence all the guns in the whole system of fortifications at the beach by taking it from behind.

It would not be a piece of cake, is what they thought to themselves on hearing the details of their adversary: two sets of four six-inch guns, a network of barbed wire, profusely reinforced concrete, the Blockhaus, *"chevaux de frise"* (anti-cavalry barriers), antitank ditches, flamethrowers and some stretches of mine fields. Not to mention 20 mm guns, a bunch of machine gun nests sweeping in unison and two batteries of heavy guns facing the sea. And as if this were not enough, the Germans had razed the lovely casino, a great tourist attraction before the war, and had built a heavily fortified blockhaus (huge bunker) on its foundations,

For the landings, the 1st *BFMC* radio team will be nine strong. These French Signals were trained at the British radio school with colleagues from the No.4 Commando.

"a real fortress all by itself" Philippe Kieffer later wrote in his Memoirs.

The second goal of No.4 Commando, after cleaning up all these positions was to leave them to the infantry and then meet up with the British 6th Airborne Division, who were to be dropped in the night, in order to seize two bridges to the east of the Orne, one on the river itself and the other on the Caen canal towards the sea.

In the absence of topographical indicators, at first Kieffer's men did not recognise the part of the coast where they were about to land. Luckily there was the group of chaps at Havre who pointed without difficulty to the channel of the Orne, the Orne itself and the Seine estuary to the east.

"Wow! We're landing at Ouistreham!" they had previously excitedly announced to their friends. The information spread like wildfire. If it inflamed understandable excitement and emotion among the French Green Berets, it also caused great concern within the officer ranks, which feared dramatic consequences from the leak of such information made so

Bill Millin in England among his fellow Commandos. This young piper appointed by Lord Lovat would enter history on June 6, 1944, by playing the bagpipes during the taking of the bridge between Bénouville and Ranville, known as code name "Pegasus Bridge".

Sunday, June 4 in the afternoon, Lord Lovat assembled his men on the lawn at Camp Titchfield. Recognisable for being decked out like a gentleman farmer, the head of the 1st Special Service Brigade harangued his Commandos and ended with words of warm encouragement to the French contingent.

near to the launch. On their honour, the men of the 1st BFMC undertook to remain silent and not to reveal their discovery to their British comrades.

Sunday, June 4, in the early afternoon, Lord Lovat gathered all his troops around him on the grass at Titchfield Camp. Wearing a gentleman farmer waistcoat over a white shirt, his hands in the pockets of his corduroy trousers, the leader of the 1st *Brigade de Commandos* (1st Commandos brigade) ended his sermon with a few words in the language of Molière *"Messieurs les Français, demain, les Boches on les aura!"* or *"Dear French Sirs, tomorrow, the Huns, we will have them!"* He said in the direction of the 1st *BFMC*.

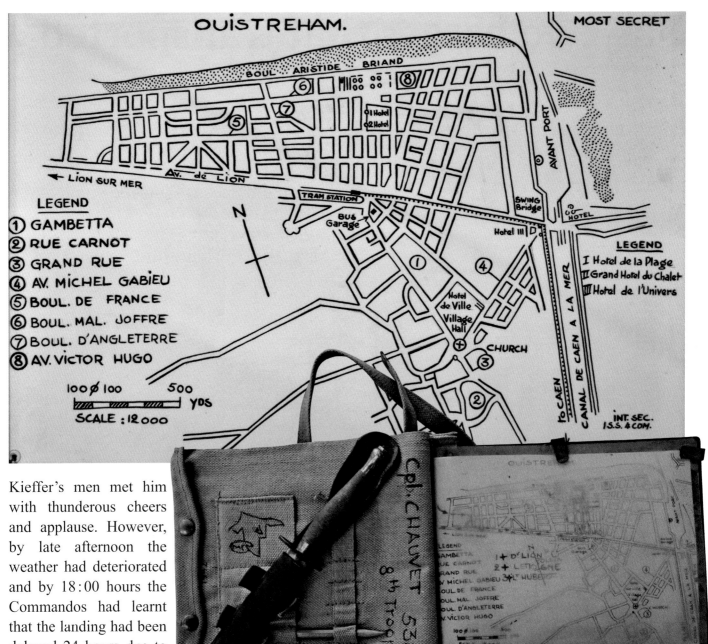

OUISTREHAM.

BOUL. ARISTIDE BRIAND

← LION SUR MER — AV. de LION

LEGEND
① GAMBETTA
② RUE CARNOT
③ GRAND RUE
④ AV. MICHEL GABIEU
⑤ BOUL. DE FRANCE
⑥ BOUL. MAL. JOFFRE
⑦ BOUL. D'ANGLETERRE
⑧ AV. VICTOR HUGO

100 Ø 100   500
SCALE : 12 000   YDS

N

TRAM STATION
BUS Garage

Hotel de Ville Village Hall
⊕ CHURCH

AVANT PORT

SWING Bridge

Hotel III

To CAEN   CANAL DE CAEN A LA MER

LEGEND
I Hotel de la Plage
II Grand Hotel du Chalet
III Hotel de l'Univers

INT. SEC.
I.S.S. 4 COM.

The bag carried by Corporal Maurice Chauvet on June 6 1944, with his Commando dagger. We can see where Maurice Chauvet has traced the route of the French Commandos in red ink on this "Top Secret" map given to the men before the operation at Ouistreham.

Kieffer's men met him with thunderous cheers and applause. However, by late afternoon the weather had deteriorated and by 18:00 hours the Commandos had learnt that the landing had been delayed 24 hours due to the weather. The farewell to Titchfield Camp, its barbed wire and its sentinels, therefore took place on Monday, June 5. The Commandos mounted their covered trucks complete with their entire kit. While rolling towards the sea, they were struck by the number of military vehicles around them: Destination Warsash, near Portsmouth, to the mouth of the River Hamble, where two barges were waiting for them to transport them to the coast of France. These were LCIS (Landing Craft - for the disembarkment of troops and capable of carrying up to a hundred men).

Before shipping out, each needed to answer "*present*" to his name-call. The most teasing among them could not resist adding the malicious little phrase: "*No return ticket, please*". The previous day, all the Commandos had written their wills. Headquarters foresaw more than fifty percent losses from the combat ranks on their very first assault.

1 Troop, under the command of Lieutenant Guy Vourch, boarded aboard the 527 with Commander Kieffer and his staffing-committee, and 8 Troop took their place in the 523, under the authority of the officier de l'équipages Alexandre Lofi. The twenty-four men of the K-Gun section were divided into two small holdings measuring about thirty meters.

23

The two barges that transported

Landing Craf, Infantry, Small (LCIS): Length : 32 meters
Width : 6.50 meters
Draught : 1,10m
Maximum Speed : 15 noeuds
Armement: 2 Canons Oerlikon - 20mm
2 Vickers Machine guns - 7.7mm
Maximum Capacity : 100 men

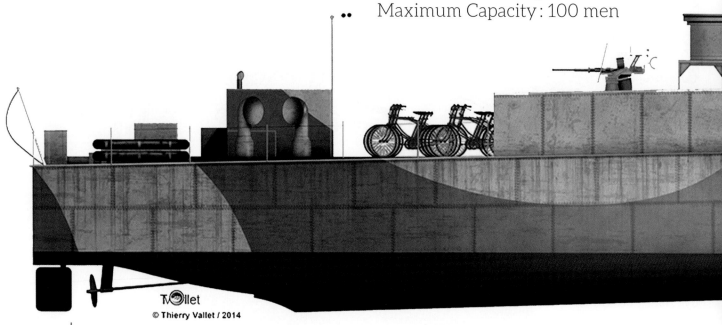

© Thierry Vallet / 2014

LCIS 523

Lieutenant Alexandre Lofi's 8 Troop : 71 men
Half of lieutenant Pierre Amaury's K-Gun section : 12 men

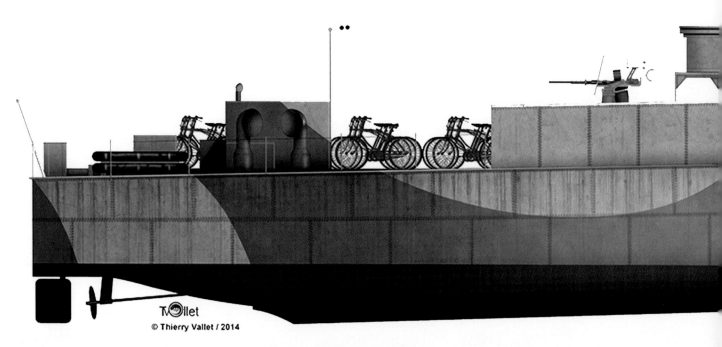

© Thierry Vallet / 2014

the 177 French Commandos

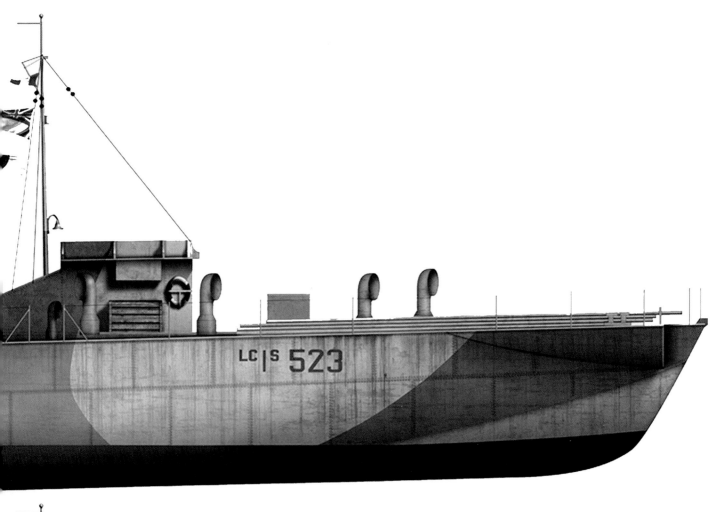

LCIS 527

Commander Kieffer and his staffing-committee: 13 men
Lieutenant Guy Vourch's 1 Troop: 69 men
Half of lieutenant Pierre Amaury's K-Gun section: 12 men

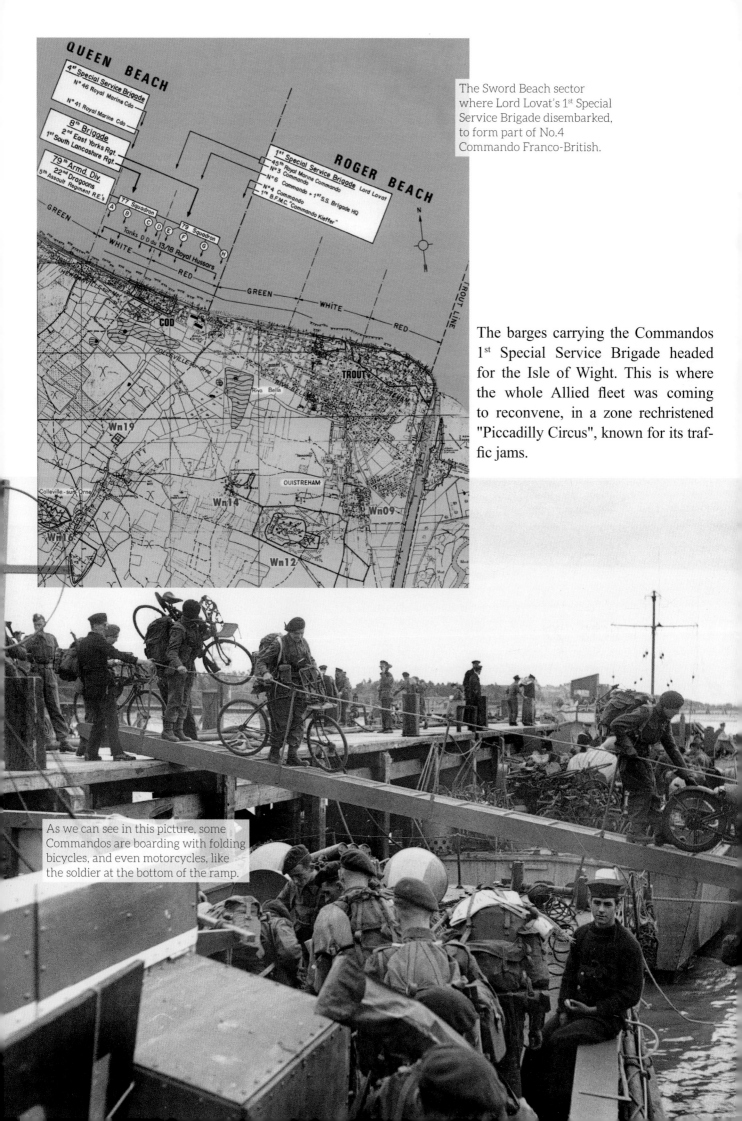

QUEEN BEACH

4ᵉ Special Service Brigade
N° 46 Royal Marine Cdo
N° 41 Royal Marine Cdo

8ᵗʰ Brigade
2ⁿᵈ East Yorks Rgt.
1ˢᵗ South Lancashire Rgt.

79ᵗʰ Armd. Div.
22ⁿᵈ Dragoons
5ᵗʰ Assault Regiment R.E.'s

1ˢᵗ Special Service Brigade Lord Lovat
45ᵗʰ Royal Marine Commando
N° 3 Commando
N° 6 Commando
N° 4 Commando + 1ˢᵗ S.S. Brigade HQ
1ᵉʳ B.F.M.C. "Commando Kieffer"

ROGER BEACH

77 Squadron

79 Squadron

Tanks D D du 13/18 Royal Hussars

GREEN

WHITE

RED

GREEN

WHITE

RED

TROUT LINE

N

COD

TROUT

Riva Bella

Wn19

OUISTREHAM

Colleville-sur-Orne

Wn14

Wn09

Wn16

Wn12

The Sword Beach sector where Lord Lovat's 1ˢᵗ Special Service Brigade disembarked, to form part of No.4 Commando Franco-British.

The barges carrying the Commandos 1ˢᵗ Special Service Brigade headed for the Isle of Wight. This is where the whole Allied fleet was coming to reconvene, in a zone rechristened "Piccadilly Circus", known for its traffic jams.

As we can see in this picture, some Commandos are boarding with folding bicycles, and even motorcycles, like the soldier at the bottom of the ramp.

One by one, the barges leave the port at Warsash to head towards the rallying point for all the allied fleet, off the Isle of Wight.

At 22:00 hours the fleet received a message from both the King of England and from Churchill: "*Good luck and God bless you.*" At this the endless convoy left "Piccadilly Circus" to move slowly towards the coast of France. Over the troubled sea, dancing in the wind bobbed the barrage balloons protecting the fleet from air attacks.

The *sous-officiers* (NCOs) of No.4 Commando prepare grenades aboard a barge in the port at Warsash, in preparation for the landings.

Aboard the barges, the atmosphere was calm, concentrated. Everyone was thinking about what he had to do, trying to ignore the presentiment of danger. Before boarding, Kieffer had warned his men that less than ten of them would return intact. With his overloaded back-pack wedged against the sides of barge 523, Leon Gautier wanted to be one of the lucky ones. He had promised his fiancée Dorothy English, whose pictured he carried in the pocket of his battle-dress, to marry her on his return.

523 barge carrying half the French Commandos leaves the port of Warsach.

Like the casino they had demolished and replaced with a bunker overlooking the beach, the Germans had profoundly changed the face of Ouistreham, a seaside resort before the war.

Located fifteen kilometers from Caen, Ouistreham Riva-Bella was before the war a famous seaside resort, as well-known for its long sandy beach as for its elegant villas overlooking the sea and the casino close to the shore. A place that had boomed since 1936 with the advent of paid leave. The arrival of the Germans from 19 June 1940 would significantly change the layout of the town and its surroundings. From the beginning, by realising the importance of the place at the mouth of the Orne, not far from Le Havre, the occupying forces had installed Flak pieces on either side of the city, then a selection of field artillery at the southern heights of Colleville-sur-Orne (now Colleville-Montgomery).

The year 1942 marked the beginning of the construction of the Atlantic Wall by the Todt Organisation. Ouistreham had become a no man's land to a depth of four kilometers, where all movement was controlled by the *Feldgendarmerie*.

On the waterfront, the Germans destroyed more than a hundred villas to create a defence barrier consisting of not less than 80 concrete structures and twenty pieces of artillery of various calibres, some under an

The men of the 736 Infantry Regiment, patrolling off Ouistreham on board a requisitioned French trawler.

For defence of Ouistreham, the Germans had about two thousand men from an infantry regiment, Infantry-Regiment 736.

Sailors from the *10. Räumboots-Flotille*, based at Ouistreham.

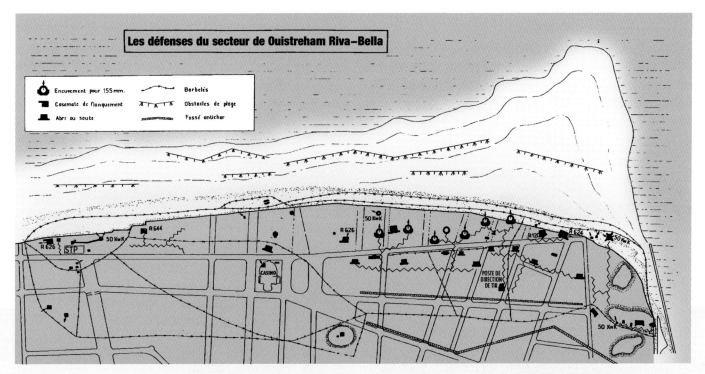

Encuvement pour 155 mm.   Barbelés

Casemate de flanquement   Obstacles de plage

Abri ou soute   Fossé antichar

R 644
R 626
50 KwK
R 626
STP
CASINO
R 626
50 KwK
R 120
R 624
50 KwK
POSTE DE
DIRECTION
DE TIR
50 KwK

armoured casemate. The biggest guns had a range of over 20 kilometers. Two underground caverns along the beach provided service for this whole ensemble, where provisions were made for staff shelter, food stocks and ammunition, not forgetting a bakery and vehicle maintenance workshop. The necessary power was supplied by a bunker with a generator. Amid this array stood the Observation Post, visible from afar, and which acted as a surveillance base to direct fire, and radio and telephone station (see pages 32 and 33).

The Germans had razed to the ground a good hundred villas to transform the seafront into a fortress.

A wide and deep antitank trench protected its fortifications to the south. The beach itself was riddled with obstacles of all kinds intended to impede the progress of the assailants: barbed wire, mines, concrete tetrahedrons, "Rommel's asparagus" (wooden stakes with pointed ends) and various traps. A second line of antitank defence consisting of "dragon teeth" concrete was placed within the enclosure.

This bunker constructed near the gazebo would cause many problems for Kieffer's men during the attack on the casino.

This photo taken just after the war shows the number of obstacles of all kinds placed on the beach.

This transformation of the resort into a fortress would be fatal to the elegant casino that had been such a joy to its guests. On account of its very useful location, in 1943 the Germans decided to raze it to the ground, only keeping the sub-soil reinforced by pouring concrete over it, at the top of which was installed a "tobrouk" (the placing of combat concrete and thereby providing an opening for a shooting range of 360°) for the MG 42 machine guns and a piece of 20mm Flak pivoted on a cement base. In addition, there were deadly MG 42s waiting in the basements.

Based on aerial photographs revealing his large area, the allied intelligence services, also intrigued by its flatness lacking much relief, would make this "casino German-style", a priority for the forces about to operate at Ouistreham.

A second large battery was built around the water tower, on the road to Saint-Aubin-d'Arquenay. Protected by an extensive minefield, it was also connected to the Observation Post. As for the port, which hosted five minesweepers and escorted the *10.Räumboots-Flotille*, it was protected by a variety of large guns pivoted on concrete bases, casemates and a "tobrouk".

To defend the sector Ouistreham, the Germans could rely on a staffing of approximately 2000 men, including an infantry regiment (*Infanterie-Regiment 736*) and a coastal artllery group from the land forces (*I./1260 Heeres-Künsten-Artillerie-Abteilung*).

Appointed Inspector General of the defences of the West by Hitler in November 1943, Marshal Rommel made two inspections in Ouistreham before the landing, on May 9 and May 30. During this last visit he attended a demonstration of rocket launchers organised for him.

A noisy demonstration of force with just one week to D-Day.

The Casino before the war; built in the 1930s, it was set right on the beach.

As can be seen by comparing these two photos, the Germans did not retain much from the original Casino.

A bunker seventeen meters high to direct all batteries

Assigned to the Todt Organisation, the site of the Observation Post had been started in September 1943 and completed in mid-November of the same year. The equipment, meanwhile, was in place shortly before D-Day. Contrary to other bunkers where the casing was made of wood, the Surveillance Post at Ouistreham was built using a special formwork shuttering technique. The workers mounted two walls with concrete bricks, then inserted metal rods and poured in the concrete, with the walls themselves serving as the formwork. It became a *Sonderkonstruction* (*SK*), no standard plan was utilised, contrary to the majority of the bunkers of the Atlantic Wall.

Measuring 17 meters high, this bunker enabled the observation of the bay of the Seine within a radius of 50 km.

As can be seen in this reconstruction, identical *in situ*, the first level was entirely underground and comprised of a room housing the 'groupe electrogene' generator and a room where the filters and air pumps were installed.

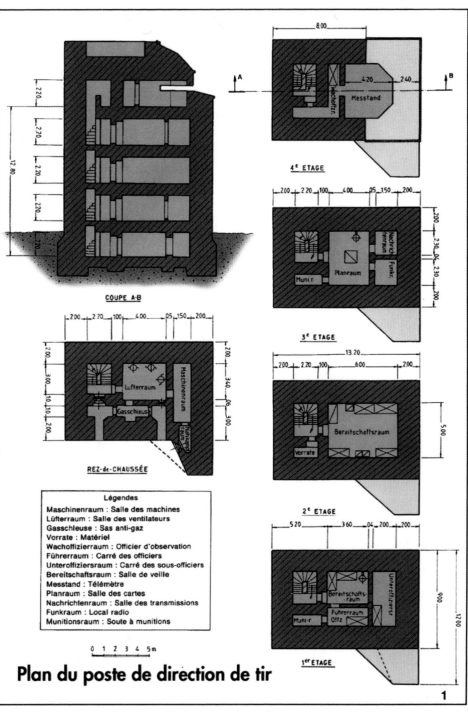

Plan du poste de direction de tir

COUPE A-B

REZ-de-CHAUSSÉE

Lufterraum, Gasschleus, Maschinenraum, Wachoffizierraum

4ᵉ ETAGE

Wachoffiz., Messtand

3ᵉ ETAGE

Muni.r, Planraum, Nachrichtenraum, Funkraum

2ᵉ ETAGE

Vorrate, Bereitschaftsraum

1ᵉʳ ETAGE

Muni.r, Bereitschafts-raum, Führerraum Offz, Unteroffizierscr.

Légendes
Maschinenraum : Salle des machines
Lüfterraum : Salle des ventilateurs
Gasschleuse : Sas anti-gaz
Vorrate : Matériel
Wachoffizierraum : Officier d'observation
Führerraum : Carré des officiers
Unteroffiziersraum : Carré des sous-officiers
Bereitschaftsraum : Salle de veille
Messtand : Télémètre
Planraum : Salle des cartes
Nachrichtenraum : Salle des transmissions
Funkraum : Local radio
Munitionsraum : Soute à munitions

0 1 2 3 4 5m

The bunker housed technical installations (a machine room, ventilation) an armoury, the personnel facilities (dormitories and infirmary), a Command Post with telephone exchange, local radio, an observatory and a telemetry station.

All of the batteries at Ouistreham and the surrounds were in radio and telephone contact with the Observation Post.

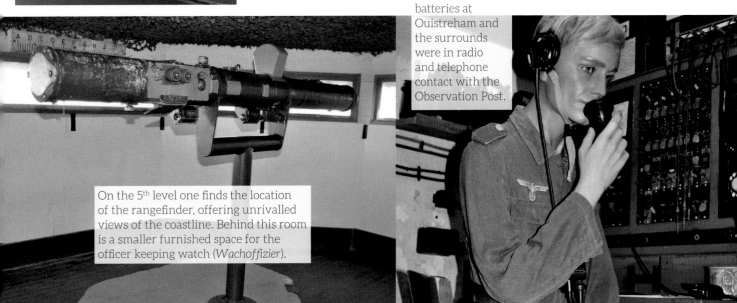

On the 5th level one finds the location of the rangefinder, offering unrivalled views of the coastline. Behind this room is a smaller furnished space for the officer keeping watch (*Wachoffizier*).

Dawson lets the French make the first landing

After a short night on the stormy sea, the barges of No.4 Commando were in sight of their goal. Hardly had they approached when a shell struck from the front of the 527, causing the first losses among Kieffer's men.

It was five o'clock in the morning when a sailor came to wake the soldiers on board. Despite the rough seas and the discomfort, the majority had been able to sleep, as is the privilege of youth. It was difficult to believe it was June. It was cold and everything was grey, vessels and superstructures of ships extended in unison to out of sight on the frothy waves. "*It was the twilight of the morning*" a Breton named Gwen-aël Bolloré later reminisced, he was not yet 19 years old and part of the medical team led by captain Lion [1]. In order to spare his family the worry, Bolloré had enlisted in the Commandos under the pseudonym of Bollinger, named after his favourite brand of champagne. After breakfast was quickly downed, each party checked their weapons and ammunition once more. During the night they had distributed a map of Ouistreham to the Commandos, so that they could finally discover the French names of their objectives. They needed to land about five hundred meters to the east of Ouistreham, at a place called "La Brèche", the locality of Colleville-sur-Orne (now Colleville-Montgomery).

Barge 519, which transported Lord Lovat and his piper Bill Millin, one can see the other LCI (S) sailing towards Normandy.

Of the same 519 barge, another view of the flotilla of the 1st Special Service Brigade.

Once on the bridge, the men were seized with the same emotion as the night before. Before their eyes were buildings of all kinds and sizes: barges chock full of soldiers, tanks or trucks, there were destroyers, frigates, battleships, sloops, minesweepers, cargo ships, tankers, tug-boats, armed fishing boats, hospital ships, liners from another age...

In all, more than five thousand ships had been requisitioned to become the largest and most motley armada of all time, almost constantly flown over by hundreds and hundreds of different aircraft: the DC 3 carrying parachutists had succeeded the bombers and fighters sent in to support the troops coming in from the sea.

Commander Kieffer lined his men up on the deck of the 527, wearing backpacks and well kitted out for the "big party". A few minutes later, while the fleet was still eight kilometers from the coast, a roar like the world was ending was unleashed without warning. At the same moment, the artillery pieces from five thousand ships were unleashed. To the soldiers it was just a dreadful noise that drowned out the sound of the engines. Positioned behind the barges, heavy Allied war-machines were on a mission to annihilate the powerful German batteries at Le Havre and at the mouth of the Orne. Brusquely awoken, the enemy

gunners began to respond. Framed by water spray, the barges nevertheless continued to advance just as in the exercise, straight for the coastline that they still could not distinguish.

While the convoy was only a few hundred meters from the shore, Colonel Dawson permitted a slight advance by both of the French barges, which were now lined on the coast about fifty meters from each other, in defiance of the shells and machine gun fire. Suddenly, through the smoke that mingled with the morning mist, the 177 French Commandos were eventually able to distinguish a thin dark band, right in front of them: France itself, their homeland. They were so moved they had trouble taking in the full measure of the drama being played out a short distance away: the sinking of a Norwegian destroyer that was capsizing vertically into the water and like a perfectly choreographed ballet, the lifeboats shuttled between the wreck and a large convoy of troops.

One hundred and seventy seven men out of the 30,000 who needed to land on Sword Beach, was not many. And it may even seem ridiculous when you consider that more than 150,000 soldiers were preparing to get a foothold on all the beaches (Utah, Omaha, Gold, Juno and Sword) across a front of about 80 kilometers.

As one can see in this photo, besides their mediocre sea faring ability, the LCI (S) had the inconvenience of tenuous evacuation because of their ramps.

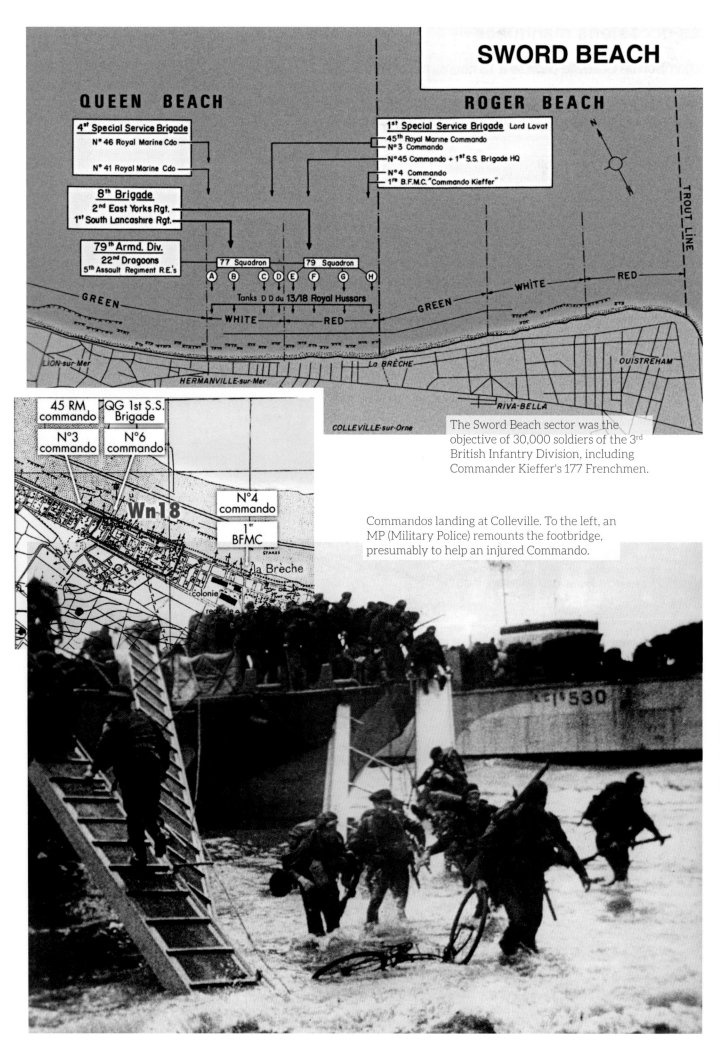

SWORD BEACH

QUEEN BEACH

ROGER BEACH

4ᵉ Special Service Brigade
N° 46 Royal Marine Cdo
N° 41 Royal Marine Cdo

8ᵗʰ Brigade
2ⁿᵈ East Yorks Rgt.
1ˢᵗ South Lancashire Rgt.

79ᵗʰ Armd. Div.
22ⁿᵈ Dragoons
5ᵗʰ Assault Regiment R.E.'s

1ˢᵗ Special Service Brigade Lord Lovat
45ᵗʰ Royal Marine Commando
N° 3 Commando
N° 45 Commando + 1ˢᵗ S.S. Brigade HQ
N° 4 Commando
1ʳᵉ B.F.M.C. "Commando Kieffer"

77 Squadron   79 Squadron

Ⓐ Ⓑ Ⓒ Ⓓ Ⓔ Ⓕ Ⓖ Ⓗ

Tanks D D du 13/18 Royal Hussars

GREEN   WHITE   RED

GREEN   WHITE   RED

TROUT LINE

LION-sur-Mer   HERMANVILLE-sur-Mer   La BRÈCHE   OUISTREHAM
RIVA-BELLA
COLLEVILLE-sur-Orne

The Sword Beach sector was the objective of 30,000 soldiers of the 3ʳᵈ British Infantry Division, including Commander Kieffer's 177 Frenchmen.

45 RM commando   QG 1st S.S. Brigade
N°3 commando   N°6 commando

Wn18

N°4 commando

1ᵉʳ BFMC

La Brèche
colonie
redoute

Commandos landing at Colleville. To the left, an MP (Military Police) remounts the footbridge, presumably to help an injured Commando.

LCI 530

But the symbolic value is undeniable. Certainly Kieffer's Commandos were not the only French natives engaged in the enormous Operation Overlord, there were also FAFL aviators and the marines of the FNFL, but they were the only ones who would participate in the terrestrial engagement, even though they were not the first to touch French soil as liberators. During the night, 36 French paratroopers, members of the Special Air Service, were dropped in Brittany. Among them Corporal Emile Bouétard had been killed in action between midnight and one o'clock on Tuesday June 6, in the Morbihan.

Advancing a few meters further and the beach defences were beginning to appear, columns and chevaux de frise entanglements, interspersed with barbed wire. Still on board the 523, Léon Gautier adjusted his green beret one last time. Like most of his comrades, he wanted to keep hold of it during the landing. The flat helmet he carried was attached from behind with elastic, he knew that he would need it later; this was as much as for protection as to avoid it bothering him during his exploits.

On the 527, Maurice Chauvet, the liaison agent, created astonishment among his comrades by checking for the last time that his folding bicycle was working properly.

There was a slight bump and the barges were halted at just a few hundred meters from the strike, at about 7.30am. With a sure and swift movement the sailors deployed the footbridges on each side of the

In this photo, you can clearly see piles driven into the sand and tetrahedrons arranged to hinder the landings. On the beach, a tank is burning.

bow and the first men flocked onto the beach, ignoring the whistling of the shells and the incessant barking of the machine guns. Before jumping into the water in his turn, Léon Gautier, with his heavy Thompson sub-machine gun at arm's length, noticed a shell hitting the front left side of the neighbouring barge that also supported the ramps. It made in a terrible noise and wounded several men, including Lieutenant Pinelli who had his legs riddled with shrapnel. Those who had not been hit then rushed to disembark on the intact bridges of the 523 that had just been coupled.

Fortunately, the British sailors had deposited their passengers at the designated place. Right before the Commandos on the other side of the beach, one could even distinguish the former holiday camp, now in ruins, that was to be their rallying point. Finding the correct positioning was crucial: a few hundred meters more to the left or to the right and Kieffer's men would have fallen into fortified German positions.

"Bent on avoiding the bullets that were coming from everywhere, I ran with all my strength straight ahead across the sand. I had not forgotten the orders: as soon as possible get yourself to the protection of the sand dunes, even regardless of the dead and wounded. My Tommy Gun was ready to fire, I stuck to Lieutenant Lofi like a shadow, "You. Follow me everywhere, I need you with your gun" my chief had reminded me just a few minutes before that fateful moment. We had been so well prepared for this attack I was not surprised how it was unfolding. The only difference to the training, so far, was the bodies of my friends that were beginning to litter the beach, among the funnels bombs, barbed wire and anti-tank obstacles", Léon Gautier later recalled [2].

Soon after landing on the sand, the French were shot at from a little bunker located to their left. Flesch, Casalonga, Rousseau, and Reiffers Piaugé Dumenoir were

Lord Lovat (who is walking alone to the right of the column) and the staff of the 1st Special Service Brigade landing at "La Brèche", about an hour after the first wave of assaults. Tanks halted by enemy fire litter the beach. In the foreground we see Bill Millin, Lord Lovat's piper and his bagpipes.

hit, more or less seriously. With his belly open, Sergeant Raymond Dumenoir, "Pepe" to his men, entered his death throes without even a complaint.

Other men would fall within the seconds and minutes that followed: Cabellan, Leostoc, Beux, Bucher as well as Lieutenant Guy Vourch, the head of Troop 1. Colonel Dawson was also affected in his turn, although wounded in the leg and head he continued to weave from one Troop to another encouraging his Commandos, wrapped in a blanket, his blond hair covered in blood. *"Go Boys!"* He shouted supportively when he recognised a fellow Frenchman. Even

Erected on the spot where the Commandos landed, this monument commemorates the sacrifice of Philippe Kieffer's men.

The Commandos are now in the dunes facing the holiday camp.

Kieffer was not spared. With a shrapnel hit to the thigh, he nevertheless continued his command after being summarily dressed by Nurse Bolloré.

The Commandos that were still standing managed to reach the cordon of the dunes topped with barbed wire, about one hundred and fifty meters from the shore. Using cutters, a gap in the barbed wire was opened by Sergeant Thubée, "*like a crown of thorns covering the face of our country crucified*" [(3)].

Even with this broken through the Green Berets were not out of the woods yet. They then needed to cross an area alleged to be a minefield. As surprising as it may seem, not a single mine would explode during their passage. The English were so surprised that they cried miracle. Léon Gautier has a more prosaic explanation: "*In fact the miracle was, I realised years later, the good fortune that a storm had blown in across*

The beach at Colleville; in the foreground, the barbed wire overhangs the cordon of dunes.

Most of the Commandos would leave their heavy
backpacks in the ruins of the holiday camp.

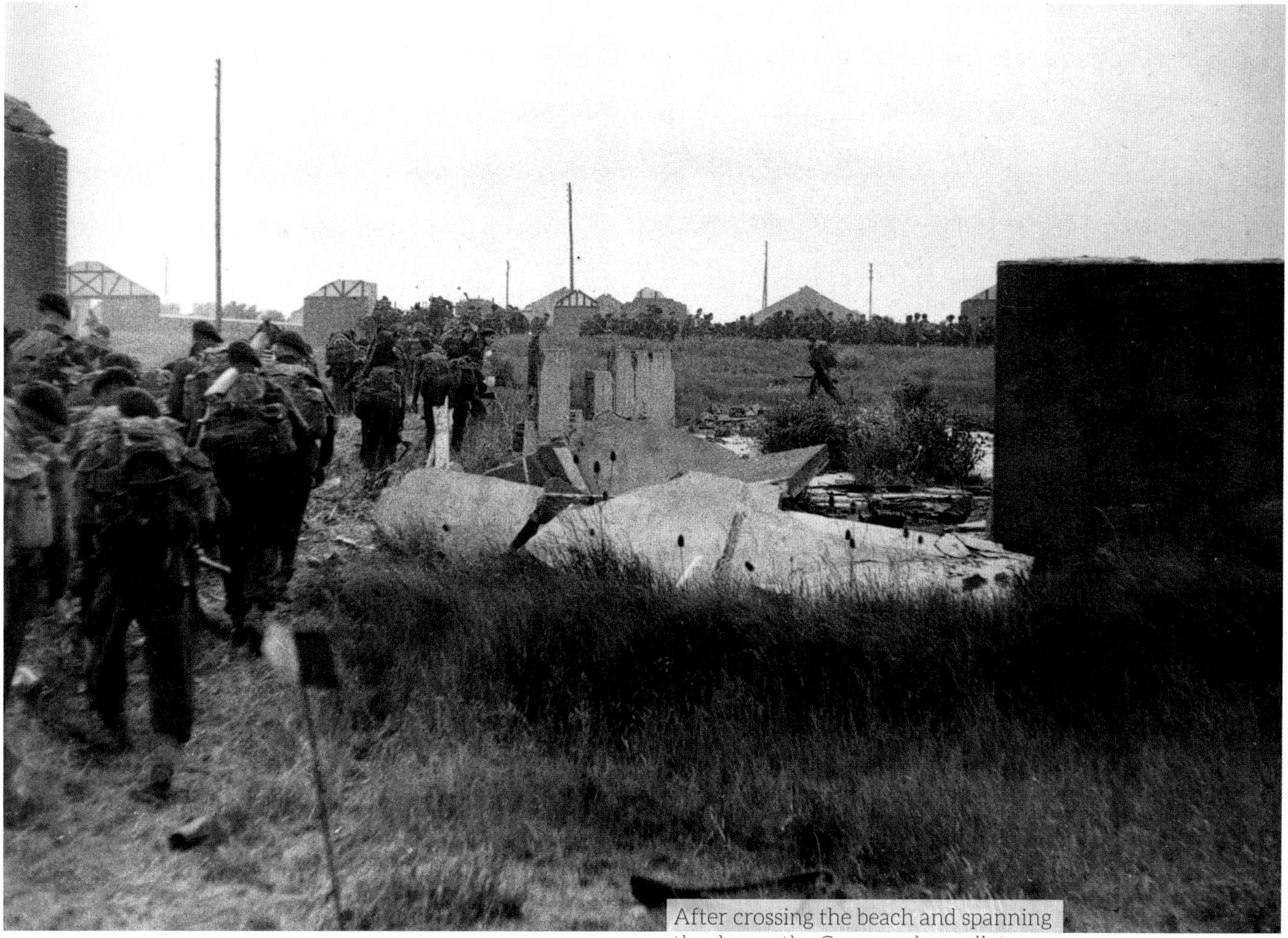

After crossing the beach and spanning the dunes, the Commandos walk to the ruins of the holiday camp, their rallying point.

the Channel just hours earlier. This had built up sand over those accursed mines, so they ended up being unusable. So what if the storm had delayed the landing by a day, it without doubt also saved the day..."[4]

Leaving their dead and wounded comrades on the beach along with tanks on fire that had landed five minutes ahead of them, the survivors of No.4 Commando had reached the ruins of the old tourist resort. Most of them off-loaded their heavy backpacks in preparation for the second part of their mission. 1 Troop had the objective of the casino that was powerfully fortified by the Germans. As for 8 Troop, it needed to reduce all enemy defences staggered along the beach and the seafront until Ouistreham. It was about 8.15am when the French Commandos left their shelter, where they had managed to revive themselves.

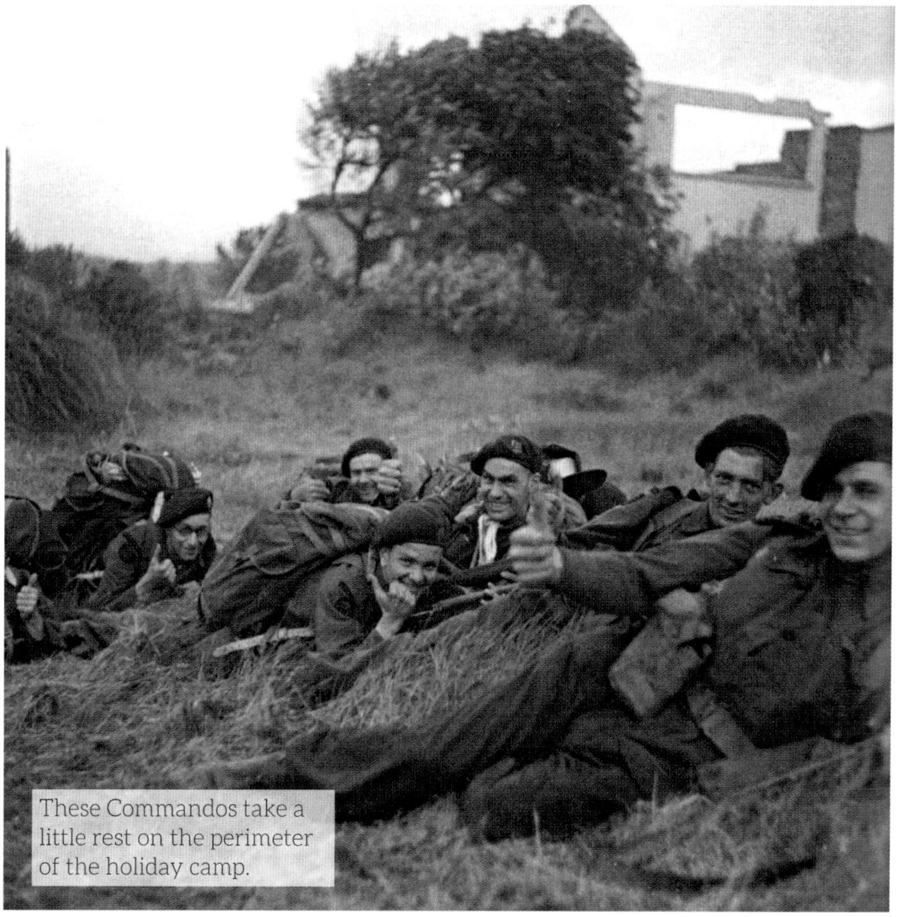

These Commandos take a little rest on the perimeter of the holiday camp.

A group of Commandos in the ruins of the holiday camp. Smiles are de rigueur before the second phase of the battle.

A Commando from the Signals in the course of using his radio in the ruins of the holiday camp.

Less than an hour after the landing, they had already counted three killed (Dumenoir, Rousseau, Flesch) and twenty-six injured, including all the officers of 1 Troop.

(1) Gwen-aël Bolloré, *Commando de la France libre*, éditions France Empire.
(2) Entretiens avec l'auteur.

The beach is under control after fighting commenced very early in the morning.

For these Commandos who are leaving the beach, the second part of their mission is only just beginning.

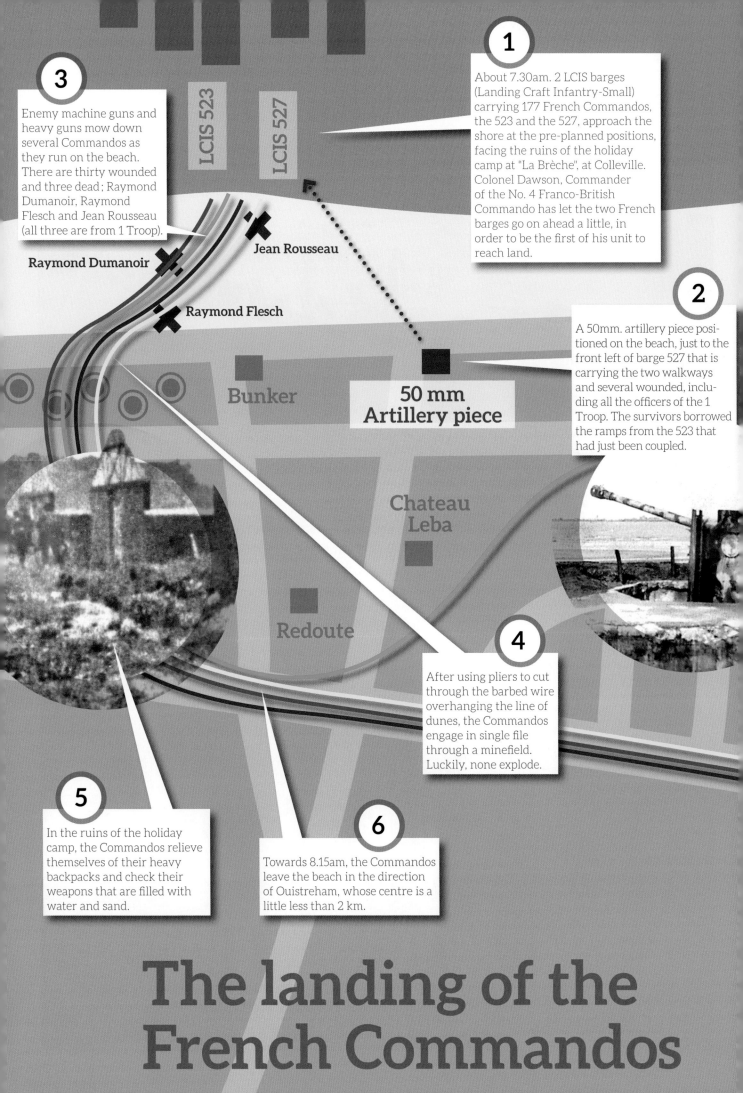

3

Enemy machine guns and heavy guns mow down several Commandos as they run on the beach. There are thirty wounded and three dead; Raymond Dumanoir, Raymond Flesch and Jean Rousseau (all three are from 1 Troop).

1

About 7.30am. 2 LCIS barges (Landing Craft Infantry-Small) carrying 177 French Commandos, the 523 and the 527, approach the shore at the pre-planned positions, facing the ruins of the holiday camp at "La Brèche", at Colleville. Colonel Dawson, Commander of the No. 4 Franco-British Commando has let the two French barges go on ahead a little, in order to be the first of his unit to reach land.

LCIS 523

LCIS 527

Jean Rousseau

Raymond Dumanoir

Raymond Flesch

Bunker

50 mm Artillery piece

2

A 50mm. artillery piece positioned on the beach, just to the front left of barge 527 that is carrying the two walkways and several wounded, including all the officers of the 1 Troop. The survivors borrowed the ramps from the 523 that had just been coupled.

Chateau Leba

Redoute

4

After using pliers to cut through the barbed wire overhanging the line of dunes, the Commandos engage in single file through a minefield. Luckily, none explode.

5

In the ruins of the holiday camp, the Commandos relieve themselves of their heavy backpacks and check their weapons that are filled with water and sand.

6

Towards 8.15am, the Commandos leave the beach in the direction of Ouistreham, whose centre is a little less than 2 km.

The landing of the French Commandos

map: Paul Gros

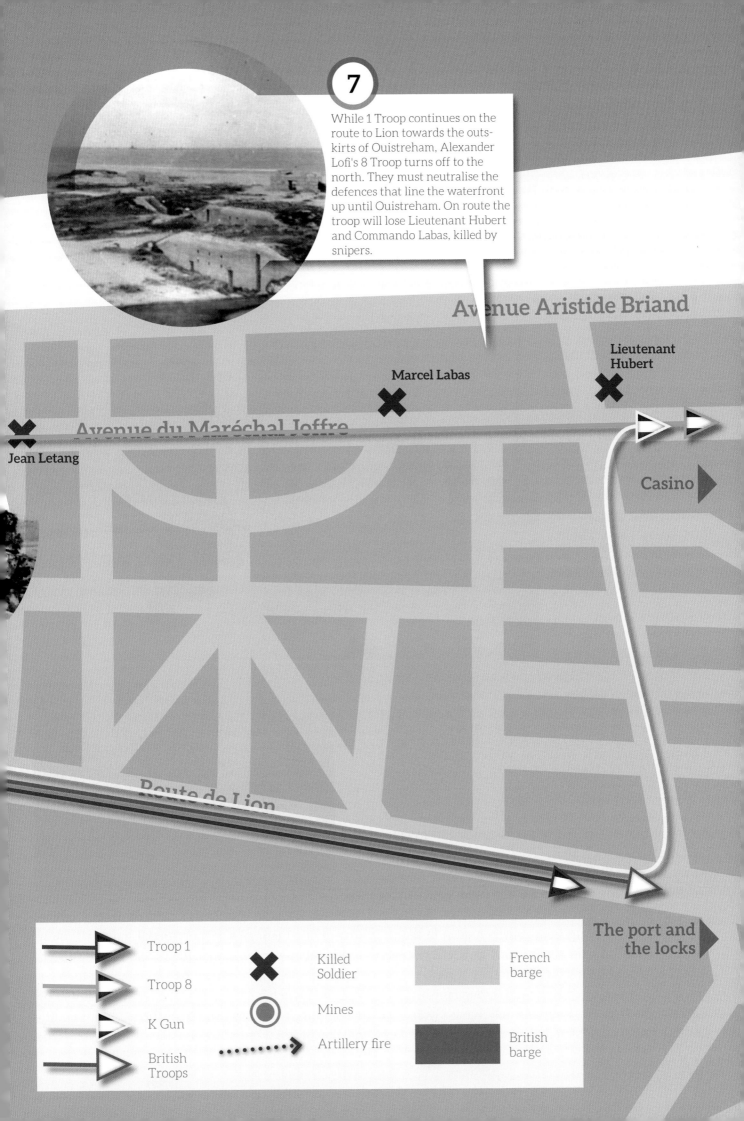

7

While 1 Troop continues on the route to Lion towards the outskirts of Ouistreham, Alexander Lofi's 8 Troop turns off to the north. They must neutralise the defences that line the waterfront up until Ouistreham. On route the troop will lose Lieutenant Hubert and Commando Labas, killed by snipers.

Avenue Aristide Briand

Lieutenant
Hubert

Marcel Labas

Avenue du Maréchal Joffre

Jean Letang

Casino

Route de Lion

The port and
the locks

➤	Troop 1	
➤	Troop 8	
➤	K Gun	
➤	British Troops	

✖	Killed Soldier
◎	Mines
┄┄➤	Artillery fire

| | French barge |
| | British barge |

After being relieved of their backpacks, the French Commandos charged towards Ouistreham, where they must neutralise the defences punctuating the sea-front and seize the heavily fortified casino. There are nearly two kilometers without a promenade.

The first half hour on French soil passed so quickly that Kieffer's Green Berets had barely noticed their soaked clothing hanging on their shoulders which were aching under their backpacks, loaded with more than thirty kilos of food and equipment. Following orders, they had left the first dead and injured behind them on the beach. With their heavy tyrolien rucksacks put aside, their armaments swiftly cleaned of sand and checked, they restarted towards Ouistreham. They had nearly two kilometers to go to reach the town centre.

Shortly after 8:00am, after leaving the beach and crossing the park at the Château Lebas, the men of No.4 Commando progressed along the Lion road in the direction of Ouistreham.

After a short journey together, Lofi's 8 Troop forked off towards the north, followed by K Gun section. Through Boulevard Maréchal Joffre, parallel to the sea, it headed towards the line of dunes to remove the coastal defences that continued to fire on the Allied fleet. Along the way, several Commandos were shot down by mortar fire, such as Couturier and Letang, the latter dying soon after.

Now overrun, the machine gun nests and bunkers would be cleared one after the other, using submachine guns, grenades and even flamethrowers for the more resistant. But the firing from snipers hidden in the remaining villas brought new victims to Kieffer's men. After Labas and Lemoigne, Lieutenant Hubert was in turn fatally struck by a bullet right through the head.

Braving the fire, Dr. Lion and his nurse Gwen-Aël Bolloré provided first aid to the injured then they

Photo taken at the same place 70 years later.

entrusted them to the British medical rescue teams, after giving them jabs of morphine. Lion and Bolloré also left their nursing colleague Bouarfa on the beach, hit by shrapnel. In a ruined house, father René Naurois, the French battalion Chaplain, gave communion to some Irish soldiers who had stopped him on noticing his pectoral cross.

Protected by DD amphibious tanks (Duplex Drive) the British Commandos infiltrate the town in the direction of the harbour and locks.

Meanwhile, 1 Troop marched towards Ouistreham by the Lion-sur-Mer road, followed by four British Troops charged with taking the port and the locks. The progress continued by following along the tram lines. Despite German fire, the column took less than forty minutes to reach the heart of Ouistreham, now evacuated by a large part of its population, but the few people left behind warmly welcome these fighters that they first took to be British.

Smiling, the men of the French K-Gun section precede the tanks at Ouistreham. First from the left is Yvan Monceau and third is Francis Guezennec.

"*What misery are we going to suffer when you leave!*" said a couple of civilians on coming across the Commandos, believing it to be like the raid on Dieppe, two years earlier.
"*We are not leaving. This time it's for good*", Léon Gautier replied to them. While a group took up position at

the intersection of Rue Pasteur and the road to Lion, the other, commanded by Guy de Montlaur, started towards the large bunker located at the other end of the street, perpendicular to the sea. This construction, at barely five feet tall, had been built on the ruins of the grand Casino that the Germans had entirely razed to the ground. All that was kept were the foundations and sub soil. Only the broad staircase and two access ramps still reflected the original glory. Its low, rounded silhouette made this fortification blend in among the dunes planted with marram grass. Its access was protected by a high concrete chicane of two meters wide and an antitank ditch reaching until the line of forts that the men of 8 Troop were in the process of conquering at the cost of several dead and wounded.

Paul Rollin was the first to sneak into the chicane, but he would not get very far. A sniper shot him in the head as he emerged out from behind the obstacle. Dr. Lion, who had just arrived a few meters from the chicane, quickly grabbed the wounded Commando, closely tailed by Bolloré. The capitaine-medicine grasped Rollin by the legs, while the young Breton grabbed his arms.

9:00am. At the corner of Rue Pasteur and the road to Lion. The gunners take up position under the gaze of civilians. At the end of the street sits the casino, the primary objective of the French Commandos.

The same place 70 years later.

An aerial photograph showing the huge surface area, the allied staffing-committee had made the Bunker at the casino a priority, built right on the beach on the foundations of the old casino from before the war.

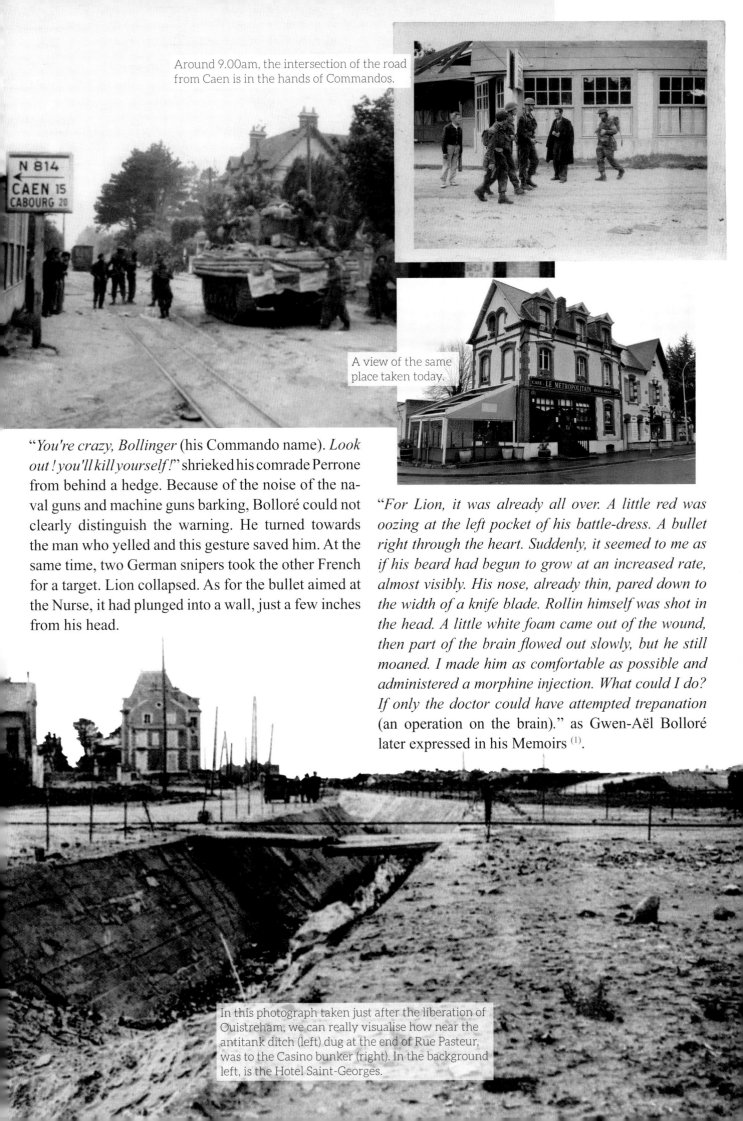

Around 9.00am, the intersection of the road from Caen is in the hands of Commandos.

A view of the same place taken today.

"*You're crazy, Bollinger* (his Commando name). *Look out! you'll kill yourself!*" shrieked his comrade Perrone from behind a hedge. Because of the noise of the naval guns and machine guns barking, Bolloré could not clearly distinguish the warning. He turned towards the man who yelled and this gesture saved him. At the same time, two German snipers took the other French for a target. Lion collapsed. As for the bullet aimed at the Nurse, it had plunged into a wall, just a few inches from his head.

"*For Lion, it was already all over. A little red was oozing at the left pocket of his battle-dress. A bullet right through the heart. Suddenly, it seemed to me as if his beard had begun to grow at an increased rate, almost visibly. His nose, already thin, pared down to the width of a knife blade. Rollin himself was shot in the head. A little white foam came out of the wound, then part of the brain flowed out slowly, but he still moaned. I made him as comfortable as possible and administered a morphine injection. What could I do? If only the doctor could have attempted trepanation (an operation on the brain).*" as Gwen-Aël Bolloré later expressed in his Memoirs [1].

In this photograph taken just after the liberation of Ouistreham, we can really visualise how near the antitank ditch (left) dug at the end of Rue Pasteur, was to the Casino bunker (right). In the background left, is the Hotel Saint-Georges.

Despite this double tragedy, Sergeant Montlaur was of course still determined to take the casino bunker, the assigned objective of the French Commandos. After considering possible locations for launching their PIAT rockets, in view of aerial photographs revealing its vast surface area Montlaur decided to position them on the first floor of a detached house, situated on the right of Rue Pasteur; he went up to there with several men. The first two shots hit the target, exploding in the doorway of the bunker. The following two rockets were precise hits.

But this was a success of short duration. While the smoke was still coming out of the casino, the building housing the rockets suddenly exploded. Throughout the entirety of his mission, Guy de Montlaur did not notice the gazebo erected in concrete on long pillars, about two hundred meters to the right of Rue Pasteur. It was from this elevated position that artillery observers had directed the fire from an 88mm. gun. If Montlaur and Lardenois had had just enough time to get out of the devastated building, Emile Renault had no chance. Hit directly by a shell, he lay dying in front of his comrades, a gaping hole in the side of his neck where you could still see his trembling organs. Ignorant of the eyes fixed on him, his lips trying to whisper something, Bolloré administered him a dose of morphine.

Thankful reinforcement for the Commandos arrived in the guise of a tall man, sporting beautiful white whiskers and a screw beret. This was Marcel Lefèvre, age 57, a veteran of the Great War and now engaged in the resistance. He informed the Frenchmen that he knew the location of the underground telephone line that connected all the German defence posts right up to Caen. Without a moment's hesitation, the Commandos walked in the footsteps of this civilian guardian angel to act forthwith, thereby isolating the bunker from the rest of the facilities.

It was about 9.30am when a tank was heard rumbling past. Believing it could be the arrival of the armoured enemy, the French Green Berets were surprised to see a British tank surge forward (A Sherman Duplex Drive or a Centaur, but on this point opinions diverge) and what's more with Kieffer in person perched near the turret.

Quickly taking measure of the situation, the "Pacha", as his men called him, sent one of the party of Commandos to search for 8 Troop to order it to attack the ghastly bunker from the other side. Directing the fire, Kieffer shot twice at the bunker, right in the bull's-eye. The enemy gun was immediately silenced. The next target was the gazebo. Four shells and the piece dissolved into nothingness. It was during this brief incident that Kieffer, while standing on the tank received his second injury of the day, on the forearm this time.

Marcel Lefèvre, a Discreet Hero

Kieffer's men owe a part of the taking of the casino to an inhabitant at Ouistreham. Marcel Lefèvre, 57 years old in 1944. A former deputy engineering officer, he had finished the Great War with five citations obtained at the front. Considered as a "French undesirable" in June 1940, he was detained in various prisons in the southern half of the country. After leaving detention, he crossed the line of demarcation (separating occupied and free France) to enter Calvados on 1 August 1941.

A fierce opponent of the German occupation, he joined the resistance, dealing in false papers and the distribution of underground newspapers, and right up until the eve of the landings provided information on German defences in the coastal zone. On June 6, he would render a great service to the French Commandos by guiding them in the taking of the casino and the gazebo, indicating in particular the location of the main underground communication line connecting all the positions of German defence, and all this in defiance of cannon and machine gun fire. "A veteran of the last war, Marcel Lefèvre, gave us information on how to reach the gazebo and avoid mines." writes Philippe Kieffer in his Memoirs.

A discreet hero, Marcel Lefèvre returned to anonymity after the war. He died in 1975.

"He spoke very little of the landings", remembers his grandson Eric Savigny, who wore the same generous moustache. "I heard him speak of it only because he had Canadian and English friends who had come to see him. I also learned that he had hid a Jewish couple in Ouistreham during the war."

The port and the locks were the objective of the British Commandos.

After the failure of the taking of the port and the locks, the DD tanks remount what is today Avenue du General Leclerc and return to their starting point at Colleville.

The route to Lion, the Commandos make a stop in front of a grocery store.

The same place 70 years later.

The last of the German defenders at the casino go up Rue Pasteur under tight escort.

The arrival of the Commandos in Ouistreham was greeted warmly by the people who had remained in the town.

Emerging from everywhere, the French Green Berets now finally reunited and made a final assault on the casino. Sensing that the place was lost, Germans toppled out in a hurry into groups from the underground area and the bunkers, their arms raised-up in surrender.

Meanwhile, the British Commandos had infiltrated the entire city under the protection of tanks. On their arrival at the port, they had wiped out a riposte so violent that it would prevent them from crossing the Caen canal to the sea.

The Commandos and 13/18th Royal Hussars tank operators fraternising with the population.

Towards 11.30 am, calm had almost returned to Ouistreham. Over the hours, the large pockets on the battle dress worn by Gwen-Aël Bolloré had not stopped swelling with registration tags; for each of them, a fallen comrade.

While the Commandos were returning to the holiday camp, taking their prisoners along they felt confidence in the British approach, as the ballet of barges and more barges reached alongside the beach. Thousands of infantrymen were landing in the footsteps of Lord Lovat's men. Had Rommel not predicted that this would be "the longest day" for the Germans as much for the Allies?...

Having replenished their arms Kieffer's men reloaded their backpacks and led a column to the outskirts of Colleville. There was no time to lose. They now needed to reach their second objective: the bridges over the Orne and the canal that should enable a meet-up with the paratroopers of the 6th British Airborne Division.

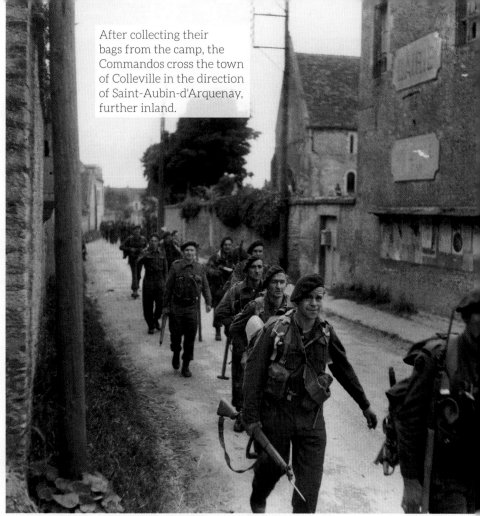

After collecting their bags from the camp, the Commandos cross the town of Colleville in the direction of Saint-Aubin-d'Arquenay, further inland.

Unlike the trajectory taken just after landing, the men of No.4 Commando this time headed towards the interior, the British preceding the French. They moved in single file, taking care to avoid mines placed in the fields bordering the road.

After the village of Colleville, they crossed the village of Saint-Aubin-d'Arquenay, now deserted by its inhabitants. Particularly exposed during this progress, the Green Berets made easy targets for crack snipers hidden in trees or in the ruins. After Wallen it was the turn of Lieutenant Amaury, head of the K-Gun section, to be injured.

Continuing south-east, after crossing a plain covered with gliders and ruptured containers from the 6th Airborne, the Commandos arrived in sight of Bénouville. They now needed to cross the footbridge. Even though General Gale's paratroopers managed to take it intact, in the night a battery of German heavy machine guns located on the towpath of the canal had still not been neutralised, and now entered into action. Hidden in a cloud of smoke, the Green Berets swarmed in small groups onto the metal structure, protected from enemy fire by the railings. Three Frenchmen were nevertheless injured during this: Derrien, Quéré and Perrone. They sheltered in Café Gondrée, near the bridge.

After crossing the second bridge, at Ranville, the Commandos moved along the water's edge until Ecarde, on the road to Cabourg. It was about 17:00 hours or 5pm when Lord Lovat arrived with his Staffing-Committe. After a brief conference, it was decided that No.4 Commando should still advance some two kilometers to the east to take up a position on the heights of Amfreville.

Once there, at about 20.00 hours or 8pm, the men in Kieffer fortified their position and dug foxholes. They

The residents of Colleville greet the Commandos as they pass.

Early afternoon: The Commandos move towards Saint-Aubin-d'Arquenay, the British are at the head and the French come along at the rear.

On the afternoon of June 6, two German prisoners being interrogated by Commandos.

took turns at the task, in groups of three. While the first handled the shovel, the second helped and the third stood guard. Indeed, the Germans were not far away and did not hesitate to let them know, "*The night was hard. Even though no serious attacks had been triggered by the enemy, however they had slipped in, in small numbers to the village and throughout the night we were vulnerable to their extremely imprecise shooting. The order was not to respond so as not to reveal the location of our automatic weapons and keep the effect of surprise in case of counter-attack in the morning*" Kieffer later related [2].

After Tuesday, June 6 1944, the 1st *Bataillon de fusiliers Commandos* would have achieved their objectives. The water-front defences at Ouistreham had been neutralised, and so had the casino, and Kieffer's men had passed along the right bank of the Orne and despite all these injuries, had more or less reached the locals who had refused to be evacuated.

The junction between the men of No.4 Commando and the paratroopers of the 6th Airborne takes place in mid-afternoon at Bénouville.

These English paratroopers posing in front of a glider may well smile. During the night, they managed to take the bridges over the Orne and hold them.

HOTEL-RESTAURANT
GONDREE
TABLE RECOMMANDEE
SHELL
HUILES CARBURANTS

This panel announces the *hotel restaurant Gondrée* which would serve as a shelter to Kieffer's injured men during the crossing of the bridge at Bénouville.

Lieutenant Bob Orrell took the "*Grand Bunker*" on June 9 in the evening, taking its 53 occupants prisoner without firing a single shot.

But at what cost... Of the 177 men who had landed twelve hours earlier, the Commandos of the 1st *Bataillon de fusiliers marins* had sixty wounded and thirty-four had to be evacuated. In addition, they already lost ten members permanently : Raymond Dumanoir, Raymond Flesch, Emile Renault, Paul Rollin and Jean Rousseau, of 1 Troop; Jean Letang from 8 Troop; Lieutenant Augustin Hubert, Marcel Labas and Jean Lemoigne from the K-Gun section; capitaine-medicine Robert Lion of the medical service. The three French Troops had had the greatest losses of all the 1st Special Service Brigade. It is understood that Lord Lovat, on the evening of this historic day, paid tribute to "*the admirable conduct and the good work of the French Commandos.*"

(1) Gwen-aël Bolloré, *Commando de la France libre*, éditions France Empire.
(2) Philippe Kieffer, *Béret Vert*, éditions France-Empire.

The "Grand Bunker": only taken by 9 June

When French Commandos left Ouistreham to take up position on the right bank of the Orne, the town was in the hands of the Allies. Well, not quite... One of the fortifications had not yet been taken, and this was by no means the least. This acted as an Observation Post, passed down in history under the name of the "*Grand Bunker*".

Their first approach to it had earned them a rain of grenades and copious machine gun fire on D-Day. The English did not persist and were focused on other objectives of higher priority, momentarily turning their backs on this impressive angular mass of raw concrete which now dominated the field full of ruins to a height of 17 meters.

But once the dust had settled on the beaches, the staffing-committee of the British engineers decided to list all the equipment abandoned by the Germans. Thus, on June 9, Lt. Bob Orrell, of the 91 Field Company of the Royal Engineers, was ordered to ascertain the contents of this work still left untouched by the fighting on June 6.

Around 22:00 hours or 10pm, Bob Orrell, a civil engineer by trade, arrived on site with three men on board a vehicle. Noting that the entrance was blocked by two huge armoured doors, the British sappers decided to put three kilos of explosives on the hinges of one of them. The explosion caused more noise than effect and it was necessary to repeat the operation by increasing the load to five kilos.

It would take a total of four hours for Lieutenant Orrell and his men to finally enter the bunker. Lit with their storm lamp, they discovered crates of grenades and other equipment on the ground floor, but not a soul was to be seen.

Suddenly, to their surprise, a male voice speaking in perfect English asked the visitors to come up. Prudently, to say the least, Bob Orrell answered that he would rather see his interlocutor come down the stairs than the reverse.

To their surprise the British witnessed the spectacle of 53 German soldiers including two officers come down the stairs and surrender themselves without the slightest difficulty.

After this surrender, which was much easier than expected, we could say that the town of Ouistreham was indeed liberated.

After two attempts to blow out the heavy armoured door, it took four hours for the British sappers to penetrate the bunker.

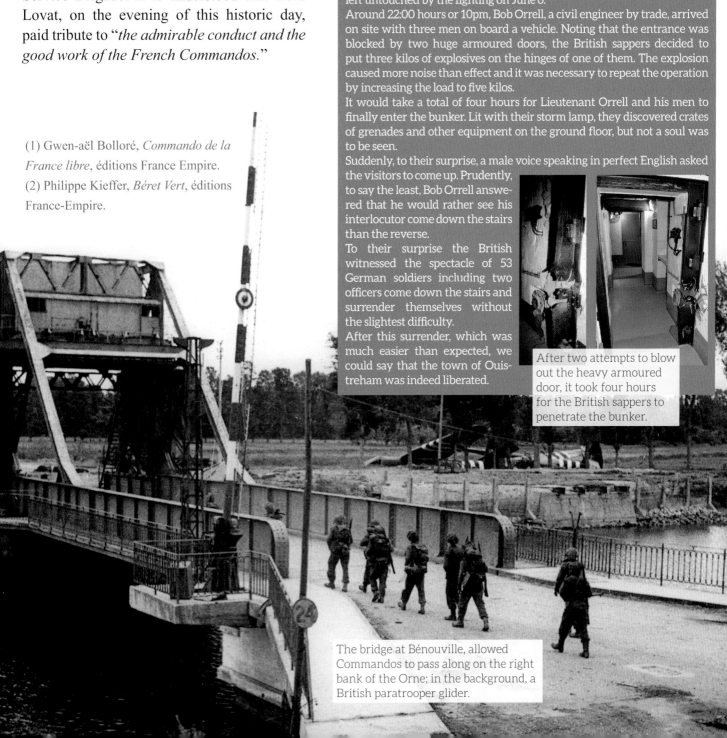

The bridge at Bénouville, allowed Commandos to pass along on the right bank of the Orne; in the background, a British paratrooper glider.

The attack on the casino

■ **Shelter**

◀ **Colleville / Orne "La Brèche"**

Avenue Aristide Briand

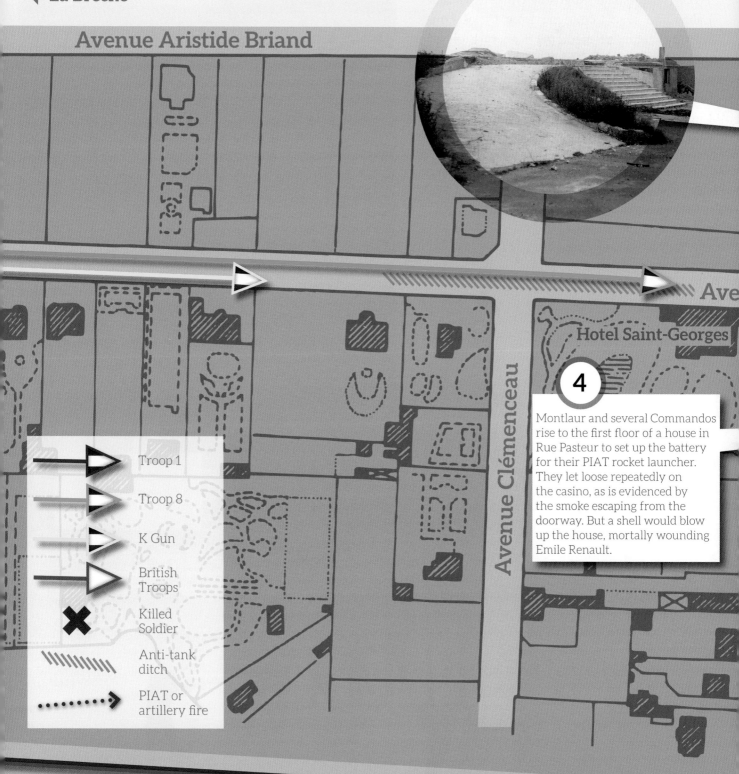

Legend:

- ▶ Troop 1
- ▶ Troop 8
- ▶ K Gun
- ▶ British Troops
- ✖ Killed Soldier
- ⁄⁄⁄⁄ Anti-tank ditch
- ·····▶ PIAT or artillery fire

Avenue Clémenceau

Hotel Saint-Georges

Ave

4 Montlaur and several Commandos rise to the first floor of a house in Rue Pasteur to set up the battery for their PIAT rocket launcher. They let loose repeatedly on the casino, as is evidenced by the smoke escaping from the doorway. But a shell would blow up the house, mortally wounding Emile Renault.

Route de Lion

map : Paul Gros

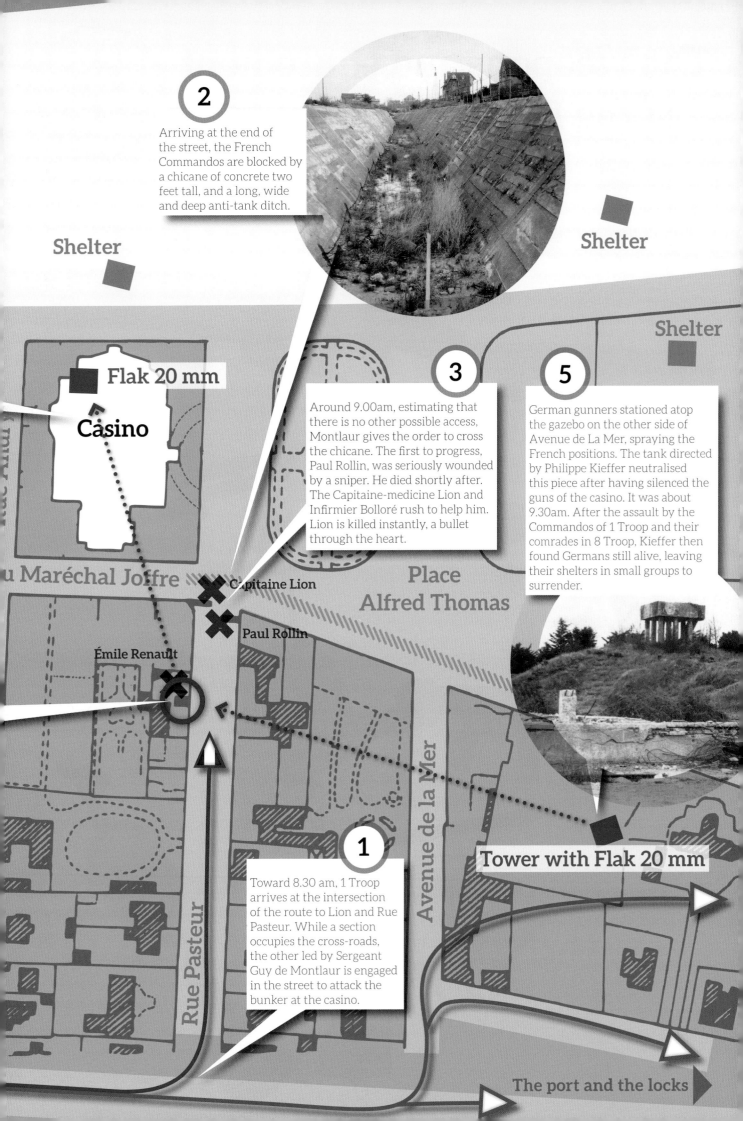

2

Arriving at the end of the street, the French Commandos are blocked by a chicane of concrete two feet tall, and a long, wide and deep anti-tank ditch.

Shelter

Shelter

Shelter

Flak 20 mm

Casino

u Maréchal Joffre

3

Around 9.00am, estimating that there is no other possible access, Montlaur gives the order to cross the chicane. The first to progress, Paul Rollin, was seriously wounded by a sniper. He died shortly after. The Capitaine-medicine Lion and Infirmier Bolloré rush to help him. Lion is killed instantly, a bullet through the heart.

5

German gunners stationed atop the gazebo on the other side of Avenue de La Mer, spraying the French positions. The tank directed by Philippe Kieffer neutralised this piece after having silenced the guns of the casino. It was about 9.30am. After the assault by the Commandos of 1 Troop and their comrades in 8 Troop, Kieffer then found Germans still alive, leaving their shelters in small groups to surrender.

X Capitaine Lion

X Paul Rollin

Émile Renault

X

Place Alfred Thomas

Avenue de la Mer

Tower with Flak 20 mm

Rue Pasteur

1

Toward 8.30 am, 1 Troop arrives at the intersection of the route to Lion and Rue Pasteur. While a section occupies the cross-roads, the other led by Sergeant Guy de Montlaur is engaged in the street to attack the bunker at the casino.

The port and the locks

The weapons and equipment of the D-Day Commandos

Like their British comrades in the 1st Special Service Brigade, Philippe Kieffer's French Green Berets landed in Normandy with armament and equipment specific to Commando Troops.

The **Lee Enfield 4 MK-1**, standard rifle of the British Army, commissioned in 1942. It would be produced in nearly five million copies during the Second World War.

The **MK 2 Sten Machine Carbine** 9mm. sub-machine gun. Fed by a right-reload 20 round magazine. Built cheaply in different versions, the Sten equipped the Home Guard, the assault troops and the *maquis* (the French Resistance).

The **Bren MK-1 Light Machine Gun**, sub-machine gun, a British Army staple. Calibre 303 (7.7mm.). Fed by a 30 cartridge; seen here with its cover and necessary maintenance equipment.

The **M 1928 A1 Thompson sub-machine gun**. Quickly renamed "Tommy Gun", this 45 calibre machine gun (11.43 mm) was supplied by 20 right-reload cartridges and was a popular weapon for the Commandos even though it was manufactured in America.

The **Webley Mark IV Revolver**, .38 calibre (9mm.). Fed by a cylinder of 6 cartridges. Reliable and popular, it was widely used by the British Army. The Commandos also used the American Colt 45 1911 (11 gauge, 43 mm.). Fed by a charger of 7 cartridges.

Ammunition for PIAT (Projector Infantry Anti-Tank), the British version of the American bazooka. With a practical range of 100 meters, the PIAT could pierce armour of all the models of tanks in service. Here we see the handled container carrying 3 projectiles.

The **fighting knife** that is the Commando's iconic weapon, so much so that it appears on the badge adorning the berets of the men of the 1st *BFMC*, designed by Maurice Chauvet.

Clip of the 5 303 calibre cartridges (7.7 mm.) for the Lee Enfield 4 MK- 1.

This French Commando is holding a rifle in his right hand; it is a Lee Enfield 4 MK-1, round his neck is the toggle rope, the all-purpose rope for Commandos. On his chest he carries two bags of circular recharges for the K-loaders rapid fire machine gun.

MK. LOT 730

Offensive Mills Grenade No.69.

Defensive Mills Grenade No.36.

The cover containing individual Commando tools, with the handle and metal forming a shovel and pick. As seen in the other photo, a metal pin on the handle secures a bayonet, thus providing an improvised tool for the detection of mines, or even a weapon for close combat.

Anti-tank mine.

Helmet with camouflage netting. Just like Leon Gautier, many Commandos disembarked wearing the Green Beret, leaving their helmets attached to their belt. Some even keep the beret on during combat in Ouistreham.

Bag with metal frame designed to carry all the impediments for the combatants. On D-Day, Kieffer's men had a good thirty kilos on their back. It is understood that they had deposited their bags in the ruins of the holiday camp before resuming the fight.

The **Commando's Green Beret**, with the distinctive insignia of Kieffer's men, designed in early 1944 by Corporal Maurice Chauvet. Seen on the shield is the brig "Adventure", the Commando's dagger and the Cross of Lorraine.

The "**Cap Comfort band**" of khaki wool, that the Commandos could use as a hat, scarf or cagoule.

Sachets of different sized bandages.

The **container** is composed of two parts. The inside upper portion holds a staple diet, the 24-Hour ration, excellent energy value in a reduced volume and limited weight. For the landing, each Commando carried two.

Box containing two bottles of water disinfection tablets.

The **individual canteen** carried by each Commando.

The **barbed wire shears**, so useful to the Commandos for escaping the beach at "La Brèche" on the morning of June 6.

Metal box containing 50 cigarettes.

The **WS 38 British manufactured radio telephone** used for liaison between smaller units. With a range of 300 to 1600m depending on the nature of the terrain, this was the Commandos No.1 radio.

From Ouistreham to Saint-Maclou, Three Months of Hard Fighting

For Kieffer's men, already well stretched at Ouistreham, the Normandy campaign would last until early September. A hundred kilometers in three months claimed new casualties of dead and injured.

On June 9, Philippe Kieffer, sick at heart, was forced to resolve to abandon his men in order to be evacuated to England, the result of D-Day injuries that had not been adequately treated. He passed the command of the 1st *BFMC* to his second officer, Alexander Lofi.

The next morning, after two days of bloody skirmishes when they fought hand to hand, the Commandos faced a violent counter-attack in the Amfreville and Breville sector. After intense mortar preparation, the Germans launched two battalions of the *21. Panzer Division SS* against Franco-British positions, confronting the three French Troops head on.

This was the beginning of the gruelling and deadly guerrilla warfare in the "bocage" hedgerows of Normandy, which would last until the end of July and at times take on the appearance of the 1914-18 War with the positions entrenched so close to each other that the enemy could easily hear them speak. In addition to artillery shelling and deadly fire from snipers hidden in the trees, Kieffer's men undergo the incessant onslaught of millions of mosquitoes that had thrived since Rommel had ordered the flooding of the valley of the Dives. In order not to be stalled in a defensive war for which they had not been trained and which was the opposite of their purpose, the Commandos conducted fighting patrols, which could also be called "harassment patrols". At night, a small group of men with blackened faces ensconced themselves sometimes up to two kilometers behind enemy lines. The Green Berets would track one behind the other, with their senses fully alert. At the slightest suspicious noise, fingers were twitching on triggers, ready to shoot. Sometimes, if the enemy did not fire, they would leave a camouflaged man at regular intervals on observation until dawn.

These patrols had the double benefit of keeping the Germans on permanent alert and made them believe there were more numerous fighters on the side of the allied guerrillas in the hedgerows.

Progression of No.4 Commando in the Normandy hedgerows, know locally as the "bocage". For Kieffer's men and their British comrades, the Battle of Normandy had begun.

In his individual battle hole, a Commando is ready to fire with a machine gun taken from the Germans.

Indeed, occupying the bridgehead over the Orne, without tanks to support the Franco-British put the 1st Special Service Brigade in precarious situation, which continually tested their physical and moral resistance. Throughout this period, the German counter-attacks were frequent and sometimes deadly. It is during the course of one of these that Guy Laot was killed on June 25. Alone against three in combat with bayonets, the "*beautiful and fearless Laot*" as Philippe Kieffer saluted him, had had time to floor two men before being hit in his turn. He was 20 years old.

"*He entered the marins fusiliers at the same time and since then we were always together. We loved to practice boxing so much ... This was not the first good friend I had lost from June 6, but never before had I been struck with such a level of grief.*" Leon Gautier would remember [1].

The efficient persistence of the Franco-British commandos would be awarded with congratulations from General Montgomery, Chief of Allied Land Expeditionary Forces. In a statement, he saluted the "*heroic tenacity*" of the 6th Division Airborne and the 1st and 2nd Commando Brigades, recalling that their resistance had enabled the 1st Corps British Army to move through the narrow corridor between the Orne and front line to engage at Caen and start their push to the southeast.

On 16 July, the same Montgomery had just personally honoured the men of the 1st Special Service Brigade, including decorating Colonel Dawson and Philippe Kieffer, who had just taken command of the 1st BFMC three days earlier.

Breville sector : Elite Commando marksmen, while camouflaged, receive their instructions before plunging into the enemy lines.

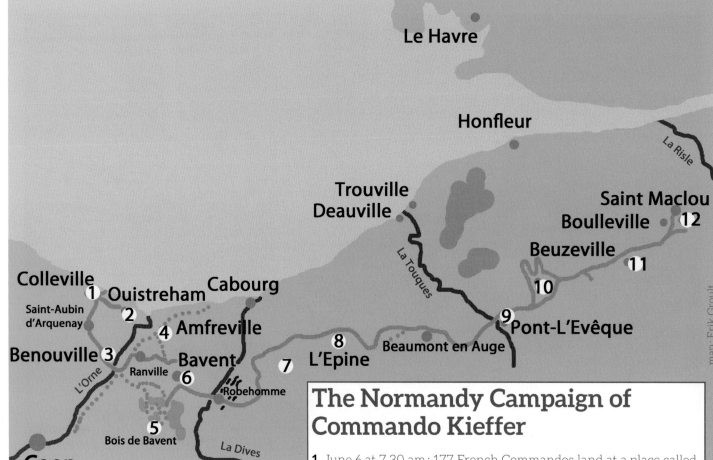

map: Erik Groult

The Normandy Campaign of Commando Kieffer

1. June 6 at 7.30 am : 177 French Commandos land at a place called "La Brèche" in the commune Colleville-sur-Orne.

2. June 6 in the late morning : fighting has ended at Ouistreham.

3. June 6 in the afternoon, they reach the canal and the River Orne and meet up with the men of the 6th British Airborne Division.

4. Line of resistance between June 6 and July 26.

5. Positions from 27 July to 16 August.

6. August 17 : the taking of Bavent.

7. Night of August 18 to 19 : crossing the flooded zones.

8. August 20 : Attack at l'Épine. Numerous prisoners.

9. August 24 : Crossing Pont-l'Évêque in flames.

10. The night of August 24 to 25 : Advanced and final combat.

11. August 26 : First contacts with F.F.I.

12. September 6 : end of the Normandy campaign.

(According to the map in the book by Gwen-äel Bolloré, *Commando de la France Libre*, Editions France Empire)

While the commandos lead the guerrillas in the countryside, the battle raged on the plain of Caen to the south.

In effect, the Germans opposed with a stronger resistance than had been expected in the attack launched by Montgomery. In addition to their 48 ton Tiger tanks, they retaliated with their formidable 88mm. guns, destroying more than a hundred British tanks. They also used new weapons like the rocket launchers known as the "Organs of Stalin".

That was why, in late July, Lord Lovat's Commandos received the order to go to the wood at Bavent, east of Amfreville, where the Germans were spraying the entire sector with "88" shots and mortars. They would spend twenty days in this extreme environment in a wood infested with mines, bombarded day and night by an invisible enemy located less than fifty meters from their positions. To be ready to strike back the men slept in their boots in trenches dug in a broken line, to avoid a shell taking them in a row.

Finally, on August 16, what remained of the 1st Special Service Brigade, about eight hundred out of an initial three thousand, rushed between the white bands which defined the secure narrow corridor across the minefields. *"To our surprise, we took the village of Bavent without firing a single shot. Germans who had occupied it had evacuated it overnight"* Léon Gautier later remembered.

June 9. The inhabitants of Amfreville quickly befriended the French Commandos. From left to right: Marcel Raullin, Guy Laot and Louis Lanternier.

Amfreville, June 9. The Australian war correspondent Chester Vilmot talks to French Commandos Marcel Raullin, Jean Priez and Louis Lanternier.

Other French Commandos at Amfreville. From left to right: Nicolas Poli, Guillaume Niclou, Otto Zivolhava, an unidentified Commando, Roland Gabriel and Louis Lanternier (half hidden).

Still at Amfreville, June 9, Guy Laot (who was killed on June 25) and Jean Priez are charmed by a little girl.

But for all that, the Normandy campaign was not over. After crossing the Dives at Robehomme, the French Green Berets and the English continued to move forward in pursuit of the Germans now retreating towards the Seine. For hour upon hour they trudged painfully on through the flooded lands infested with mosquitoes. At night, creeping silently in a single file, they managed to cross enemy lines, without arousing the attention of their sentries. And in the early hours of August 20, while about 70km to the south-west, the Germans, still in combat mode, were preparing to give a final assault in the "Falaise Pocket", the commandos went into action at a place called "L'Épine" east of the Dives. Their seizure of the German position using bayonets allowed the British infantry to arrive at the entrance Pont-l'Évêque.

The offensive was crowned a success. The French and the English had taken many prisoners among the disoriented and demoralized Germans.

On 21 August, the commando is transported to Beaumont-en-Auge, in order to re-establish contact with the Germans.

Pont-l'Évêque was in flames when Kieffer's men made their entrance. The Germans had partially burned the town down before leaving. The heat was suffocating and created a hallucinogenic spectacle. After Beuzeville in Eure, where they were welcomed as liberators, the commandos stopped at Saint-Maclou to take a well deserved rest. They had been fighting for nearly three months without respite on the front line. Since 6 June, they had travelled more than a hundred kilometers, never laying down their arms, sleeping just a handful of hours, if not just a few minutes, between attacks. Meanwhile, they learned of the liberation of Paris and the news only enhanced their determination.

On 8 September, the French berets were shipped to Arromanches on a troop transport to Folkestone. Three months and two days after setting foot on French soil, they would now travel again in the reverse direction.

Amfreville. British officers visit the Commandos.

Amfreville, July 16. Colonel Dawson, head of No.4 Commando, is also decorated by Montgomery.

After the medical evacuation of Kieffer on June 9, it was his second, Alexander Lofi who took provisional command of the 1st BFMC.

July 16, Amfreville. General Montgomery decorates the men of the 1st Special Service Brigade, shaking hands with Philippe Kieffer.

Amfreville July 14. René Naurois, Chaplain of French Commandos, celebrating Mass with the Curate of Amfreville. The inhabitants of the town join the soldiers.

Wounded in Normandy, Lieutenant Hulot returns to England. He brings back a souvenir, a German rangefinder.

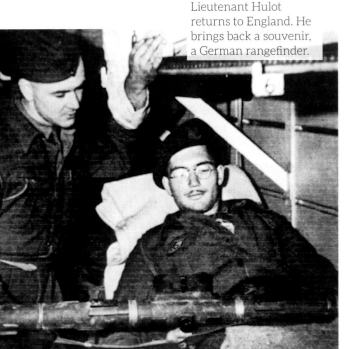

Of the 177 French Commandos who landed on June 6, only 24 finished the Normandy campaign without being injured. Twenty-one were killed. As for Philippe Kieffer, who had carried this group of men from the beginning, victory was overshadowed by tragic news. On August 25, while Paris was being liberated, his son Claude, who had joined the Resistance, was captured and shot by the Germans with a dozen fellow French resistance fighters (*maquisards*). He was 20 years old.

(1) Interviews with the author.

A British Commando reads a message from his child.

From the landings in Holland to the birth of the Marine Commandos

Nearly five months after D-Day, Kieffer's men landed on the island of Walcheren, in the Netherlands. If the first *BFMC* was dissolved in 1946, his example would give birth to the naval Commandos, spearhead of the French elite troops.

September 8 1944, Philippe Kieffer's men embarked from Arromanches for England. All of them were fascinated by the spectacle of the enormous artificial port, which continued tirelessly to land all the logistics necessary for the advancing of the troops to heart of Germany. The two Troops 1 and 8 became the 5 (Alexandre Lofi) and the 6 (Guy Vourch). As for the No.4 Commando, it was from now on part of the 4th Special Service Brigade. A month later, it was time to integrate new recruits and to re-equip, this led to the departure of the entire No.4 Commando for the Netherlands.

The objective was the island of Walcheren, neighbouring Belgium, on the south coast. The Normandy ports were now too small and too far from the front to be useful, the Allies had taken Antwerp in early September. However, they could not use their installations, although intact, because the Germans still occupied the right bank of the l'Escaut and the islands forming its estuary including that of Walcheren. Hence the operation engaging nearly 160 Frenchmen commanded by Philippe Kieffer, who also held under his command two British Troops.

Reinforced with some 600 men, the No.4 Commando landed at Flushing, south of the island, in the early hours of the 1 November 1944. The days previously, allied warplanes had bombed the dikes copiously so as to disrupt the German defences. On 2 November evening, after violent street fighting, the last points of resistance in the city were removed.

But the British and French Commandos had not yet finished their campaign in Holland; far from it. They

Shootout covering the advance of the Commandos along the waterfront of Flessingue on the Island of Walcheren.

On the waterfront at the island of Walcheren, the coming ashore of a British tank, a "flail" with chains at the front to detonate mines.

now had to go up to Westkapelle, the westernmost point of the island, where they had been called in as reinforcements. Westkapelle fell in turn on November 8, thanks to Lofi's Troop 5 who had decisively led the action against the German garrison. In the aftermath, once L'Escaut was cleared, Antwerp could welcome its first convoy until the end of the month. And, suddenly, the Allies fighting in the Ardennes and the Rhine were able to be supplied with reinforcements as required.

The No.4 Commando would stay in Holland until early March 1945, performing several night raids. Meanwhile, the first *BFMC* had grown to a third troupe that brought its soldiers up to 210 men.

On May 24, nearly three weeks after the armistice, the Green Berets were honoured in France. A detachment of the No.4 Commando, consisting of forty French

Two weeks after the German capitulation, Philippe Kieffer will have the honour of marching with Colonel Dawson at the head of the survivors of No.4. Commando Franco-British.

Philippe Kieffer died on Nov. 20, 1962. A plaque honours him at Ouistreham, recalling the important role that he and his men played in the liberation of the town.

and many British, filed into Paris under the command of Colonel Dawson and "*capitaine de corvette*" Kieffer. The 1st *Battaillon de fusiliers marins commandos* was officially disbanded on 1 April 1946. This was not an April Fool's joke nor the disappearance of the berets back to France. Rather the contrary. Kieffer's men had sufficiently demonstrated their effectiveness over the past three years to encourage the new leaders of the French army to keep on this elite young force. Thus, in the very same year, France initiated a school of marine fusiliers Commandos at the Siroco Centre, Cape Matifou, near to Algiers. Within a year, three Commando Troops would be created.

Over the years, additional Commandos were established, and the Green Berets of Kieffer would be engaged in Indochina and Algeria. In 1962, following the independence of Algeria, the centre moved to Lorient Sirocco. This was somewhat of a homecoming as the major port city has greeted the school of marin fusiliers since its inception in 1856 and until its dissolution in 1940.

The heirs of the first *BFMC* were now divided into six specialised Commandos, each carrying the name of a Commando who died in combat: Commando Jaubert (sea assault and hostage rescue), Commando Trepel (sea assault and hostage rescue), Commando Monfort (support and destruction offensive), Commando de Penfentenyo (reconnaissance and intelligence), Commando Hubert (underwater/sub-marine action).

As for the latter, it is named after the "father" of the French Commandos. Commando Kieffer was established in 2008. It specialises in the fight against new threats, such as drones and electronic warfare. These six Commandos rely on the Special Operations Command, created in 1992, placed under the orders of the Chief of Staff and under the direct authority of the President of the Republic.

Like their glorious predecessors, today's Commandos are still wearing the famous Green Beret adorned with the insignia designed in 1944 by Maurice Chauvet, except with one difference, the original title banner "1 Blion F.M. COMMANDO" has been replaced by "COMMANDOS MARINE".

Passing away in 1962, Philippe Kieffer would only see the beginning of the continuation and growth of the movement he had initiated in 1941 with a handful of volunteers. As crazy and determined as he was, the 40 year old banker without military experience had kept up his enthusiasm and energy for 20 years.

Enemies of yesterday become friends at Ouistreham

Léon Gautier, formerly of the Kieffer Commando group, and Johannes Börner, the now French former German paratrooper, both live in Ouistreham. They became friends and together they bear testimony to the horrors and absurdity of war.

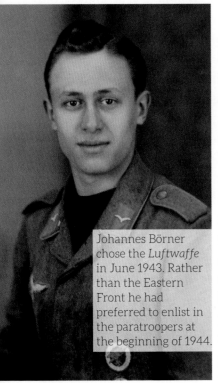

Johannes Börner chose the *Luftwaffe* in June 1943. Rather than the Eastern Front he had preferred to enlist in the paratroopers at the beginning of 1944.

Born in Rennes in 1922, Léon Gautier joined the Navy at 17. He joined General de Gaulle in June 1940.

June 6, 1944, while Léon Gautier was landing in France, Johannes Börner had set off to Normandy to take part in the gigantic battle that had just begun. Marching during the night to escape enemy aircraft from Finistère onwards, where the 5th *Fallschirmjäger Regiment* were stationed. This would be a baptism of fire for the young German paratrooper who was not yet 19 years of age and who, before the war, had dreamed of becoming a theatre actor or opera singer. Despite his inexperience, Johannes was eager to fight. Like all the men of his elite division, he was reinforced by preparation and confident that the Allies would quickly be repelled back into the sea. Besides, how could the Third *Reich* possibly be beaten despite its setbacks on the Eastern Front? Since his childhood, in Leipzig, Johannes had been educated in the Hitler cult with the certitude of the superiority of the German people. One day in April 1935, he went out of his way to convince his father to let him attend a meeting of the Führer. He returned "galvanised", finding Hitler *"even better in real life than in pictures and newsreels."* [1]

The Hitler Youth had succeeded the *Reicharbeitsdienst* (*Reich* Labour Service) before incorporation into the army. Johannes chose the *Luftwaffe* so as not to be sent to Russia. He began his training in Czechoslovakia and continued it at Blois and then in Brittany, where the harshness of the training quickly made him feel that war, the reality, was approaching rapidly. After a forced march of 350 kilometers, the *Fallschirmjäger* reached Saint-Lô on June 12 in the morning. The sight of this town, 95% of which had been destroyed gave him a taste of what awaited them. In the wake of the capture of Saint-Lô, the Allies triggered Operation Cobra. On July 25, some 2,500 planes attacked the Germans who were fleeing south and sixty thousand tons of bombs were dropped on a perimeter of 12 square km. For the "Green Devils" *Fallschirmjäger* it meant the relentless retreat to the "cauldron" at Chambois.

On 21 August 1944, completely exhausted, clothes all ragged, the survivors of the 5th Regiment of the 3rd *Fallschirmjäger-Division* were captured by the Canadians as they struggled with flagging energy, in what has been referred to from this moment as "The Corridor of Death." Johannes was caught between anger at being unable to continue fighting and relief at seeing the slaughter end. Upon his arrival at Saint-Lô, two months earlier, his company counted one hundred and twenty men. Now there were only nine still alive. Confined for the first time at the camp at Audrieu near Bayeux, in the company of six thousand other German prisoners, the young paratrooper was transferred

(1). Johannes Börner and Léon Gautier tell their life story and speak of their friendship in the book *Ennemis et Frères*, Jean-Charles Stasi.

after a year to Fleury in the Caen area. One day they assembled all the prisoners to ask if there were any farmers among them, Johannes did not pass up the opportunity to leave captivity. He did not want to end up like his fellow prisoners who were shredded during de-mining operations on the roads of the sector.

Here he was, the little guy from the big town, who had never mowed wheat nor touched the udder of a cow, finding himself in a farm near Falaise. Two long years had passed since the hell of the summer 1944. With the same application that he showed to acquire proficiency with arms, Johannes carried out his agricultural apprenticeship and learnt the French language. Over the weeks, he discovered a world less restricted than anything he had experienced before.

In September 1947 a French officer came to inform him that he now had three choices: to return to a prison camp, to return to his country which was now called East Germany, or to stay in France as a voluntary worker but subject to regular police checks.

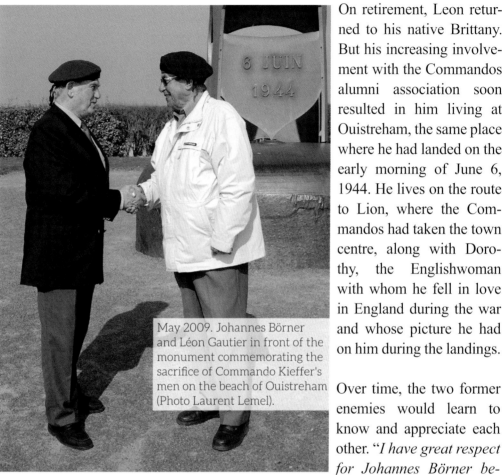

May 2009. Johannes Börner and Léon Gautier in front of the monument commemorating the sacrifice of Commando Kieffer's men on the beach of Ouistreham (Photo Laurent Lemel).

"I did not hesitate long. I knew that I could not endure confinement. I no longer had a mother. And in his letters, my father had made me aware that the Soviet regime was very hard on the population. That's why I decided to stay in France."

From this time onwards Johannes has remained. Immediately after his release, he worked as a gardener at a hotel in Lion-sur-Mer. In 1954, he met the woman who would become his wife, Therese, a beautiful blonde with blue eyes. A native of Amfreville, from very near the bridges over the Orne, Theresa had not forgotten the Green Berets of Commander Kieffer who, at the height of the fighting in the summer of 1944, were stationed at a nearby farm. Now considering France his own country, Johannes applied for citizenship. The decree arrived on March 16, 1956. In 1969 Johannes and Thérèse opened a restaurant at the centre of Ouistreham. Over the years, the Chateaubriand has welcomed veterans of all nationalities, attracted as much by the culinary talents of the patron as by the warm welcome of Johannes as their host.

This is how the former German paratrooper who became a French national met Leon Gautier: After living in England and Africa, the former Kieffer Commando finally returned to France where he worked for twenty years as an expert in the automotive business.

On retirement, Leon returned to his native Brittany. But his increasing involvement with the Commandos alumni association soon resulted in him living at Ouistreham, the same place where he had landed on the early morning of June 6, 1944. He lives on the route to Lion, where the Commandos had taken the town centre, along with Dorothy, the Englishwoman with whom he fell in love in England during the war and whose picture he had on him during the landings.

Over time, the two former enemies would learn to know and appreciate each other. *"I have great respect for Johannes Börner because he is an honourable man. He has something on his conscience, this man, but his consciousness is not that of a dishonest man. This makes him somewhat justified in having done what he did. And we must respect that"* said his friend Leon.

Despite the weight of the years, both veterans do not spare themselves to act as witnesses to the horror of war to audiences of all ages, including school children. They do this alone or together.

"After everything I've been through, I am very attached to freedom. That is why I find the memorial work important and I don't miss the celebrations that take place in Ouistreham. So that this never happens again." says Johannes who, like Leon, considers the numerous requests from French and foreign media as a "duty" that it is inconceivable to avoid.

177 French Commandos on D-Day

APPENDIX

L/Cpl. A. Allain	Sgt. R. Dumanoir	Cpl. M. Lahouze	Pvt. R. Ohliger
Lieut. P. Amaury	L/Cpl. A. Dupont	Sgt. L. Lanternier	Pvt. J. Ollivier (Guivarch)
Pvt. F. Andriot	Cpl. P. Ernault	L/Cpl. G. Laot	L/Sgt. G. Paillet
L/Cpl. A. Archieri	L/Cpl. G. Fagou	Sgt. Major A. Lardennois	L/Cpl. J. Pèrone
Cpl. A. Autin	W.O.1 H. Faure	Sgt. M. Laventure	Pvt. J. Peters
2/Lieut. A. Bagot	L/Cpl. R. Flesch	Sgt. Major M. Lavezzi	L/Cpl. R. Piauge
L/Cpl. N. Ballaro	Cpl. A. Foliot	Cpl. J. Le Bris	L/Cpl. G. Picou
Sgt. M. Barbe	L/Cpl. R. Fougere	Cpl. H. Lechaponnier	Lieut. J. Pinelli
L/Cpl. L. Bégot	Cpl. L. Fourer	L/Cpl. M. Le Floch	Cpl. J. Piriou
Cpl. A. Bernard	L/Cpl. M. Fromager	Cpl. J. Le Goff	L/Cpl. J. Plancher
L/Cpl. B. Beux	L/Cpl. R. Gabriel	L/Cpl. M. Legrand	L/Cpl. N. Poli
Cpl. J. Biestro	Cpl. R. Gadou	Cpl. J.Lemoigne	L/Cpl. L. Prévost
Sgt. P. Boccador	L/Cpl. J. Gallon	L/Cpl. R. Le Morvan	Pvt. J. Priez
L/Cpl. G. Bollinger	Cpl. M. Gannat	L/Sgt. J. Le Naour	L/Cpl. Y. Quentric
(Bolloré)	Cpl. F. Garrabos	L/Cpl. R. Leostic	Cpl. P. Quere
L/Sgt. O. Bouarfa	Cpl. J. Gauthier	L/Cpl. B. Le Reste	L/Cpl. M. Raulin
L/Cpl. G. Bouchard	(Zivohlava)	L/Cpl. A. Le Rigoleur	Pvt. M. Ravel
L/Cpl. E. Bougrain	Cpl. L. Gautier	Pvt. R. Lesca	L/Cpl. J. Reiffers
Pvt. R. Boulanger	Pvt. R. Gersel	Cpl. J. Letang	L/Cpl. E. Renault
L/Cpl. J. Bouilly	Pvt. M. Gery	Captain R. Lion	Cpl. H. Richemont
L/Cpl. A. Bourret	L/Cpl. H. Gicquel	Lieut. A. Lofi	Cpl. P. Richen
L/Cpl. G. Briand	L/Cpl. L. Godard	Sgt. M. Logeais	L/Cpl. M. Riveau
Sgt. P. Briat	Pvt. R. Goujon	Cpl. R. Lossec	Sgt. R. Roelandt
Sgt. R. Bucher	Cpl. O. Gouriou	L/Cpl. R. Madrias	L/Cpl. P. Rollin
Cpl. L. Cabellan	L/Cpl. A. Grail	Cpl. F. Magy	Cpl. G. Ropert
L/Cpl. M. Caille	L/Cpl. F. Grinspin (Grispin)	Pvt. A. Maler	Pvt. R. Rossey
Sgt. A. Cartier	Pvt. F. Guezennec	Sgt. P. Mariaccia	L/Cpl. M. Rougier
Cpl. Laurent Casalonga	Pvt. P. Giudicelli	L/Cpl. R. Massin	Pvt. J. Rousseau
Cpl. J. Cevoz-Mami	Cpl. J. Guilcher	L/Cpl. J. Masson	Cpl. R. Roux
Sgt/Mjr. P. Chausse	L/Cpl. G.Guillou	2/Lieut. J. Mazeas	Cpl. M. Rouxel
Cpl. M. Chauvet	L/Cpl. E. Guinebault	Sgt. G. Messanot	Cpl. Y. Ruppé
Cpl. P. Chouteau	Pvt. E. Guy	L/Cpl. Y. Meudal	Sgt. R. Saerens
L/Cpl. G. Coppin	L/Cpl. J. Guyader	L/Sgt. J. Moal	Cpl. G. Scherer
Pvt. M. Corbin	Sgt. G. Hattu	Pvt. R. Moguerou	Sgt. J. Senée
L/Sgt. G. Coste	Sgt. J. Horny	L/Cpl. J. Monceaux	Cpl. J. Simon
L/Cpl. J. Couturier	Sgt. J. Hourcourigaray	L/Cpl. J. Montean	L/Cpl. R. Strina
L/Sgt. R. Croizer	2/Lieut. A. Hubert	Sgt. G. de Montlaur	Cpl. P. Tanniou
L/Cpl. L. Danson	2/Lieut. L. Hulot	Cpl. J. Morel	Sgt. M. Thubé
L/Cpl. R. Dechambou	L/Sgt. R. Jovenin	Sgt. H. Nassau de	L/Cpl. E. Troyard
Cpl. P. Demonet	L/Cpl. A. Jung	Warigny	L/Cpl. C. Valentin
L/Cpl. A. Denereaz	Cpl. J. Kermarec	Captain R. de Naurois	Cpl. P. Vinat
L/Cpl. M. Derrien	Major Ph. Kieffer	L/Cpl. A. Neven	L/Cpl. M. Vincent
L/Cpl. F. Devager	Sgt. Major F. Klopfenstein	Pvt. J. Neven	Lieut. F. Vourch
L/Sgt. H. Dorfsman	L/Cpl. M. Labas	L/Cpl. J. Nicot	Lieut. G. Vourch
L/Cpl. R. Ducasse	Cpl. J. Laffont	L/Cpl. M. Niel	L/Cpl. H. Wallen

. . . .

Grades of the British Commandos and their correspondence
with the French Army and the French Navy:

Major = Commandant = Capitaine de Corvette
Cpt. (Captain) = Capitaine = Lieutenant de Vaisseau
Lieut. (Lieutenant) = Lieutenant = Enseigne de Vaisseau
1ère classe
2/Lieut. (Second Lieutenant) = Sous-Lieutenant
= Enseigne de Vaisseau 2e classe
W/O.1 = Adjudant-chef = Maître principal de 1ère classe

Sgt/Mjr (Sergeant-Major) = Sergent-chef = Premier Maître
Sgt. (Sergeant) = Sergent = Second Maître
L/Sgt. (Lance-Sergeant) = Caporal-chef = Quartier-Maître
1ère classe
Cpl. (Corporal) = Caporal = Quartier-Maître 2e classe
L/Cpl. (Lance-Corporal) = Matelot breveté = Matelot 1ère classe
Pvt. (Private) = Simple soldat = Matelot sans spécialité

The tale of the local photographer

If today we have so many pictures of Ouistreham, before, during and after the fighting on D-Day, a large part of it is due to an inhabitant of the town.

Son of a photographer, Jean Lesage, had all the necessary equipment, including the scarcely available film, to capture these moments in history. It was he who took the pictures of Kieffer's men entering the city and fraternising with the population, more than surprised to hear these French speaking soldiers wearing British uniforms. It was he who again captured the gutted casemates, the barges stranded on the shore, and the bomb craters as vast as ponds. It was he who followed with his camera the huge clearance and

reconstruction of this old seaside resort, transformed by the Germans into a fortress. A fortress surrounded by a beach that had become a no-man's land full of artillery batteries and deadly traps.

In short, a key witness to whom this book owes so much.

Portraits of Jean Lesage.

Photographic equipment used by Jean Lesage.

A barge wrecked
on the sands.

A firing position with
a recuperated French
tank turret; seen in the
background barriers
and obstacles designed
to hinder landings.

The impacts on bunkers
attest to the violence
of the fighting on the
beach.

The Observation Post, as seen
from a bunker that was under
construction.

The sector with the casino just after the war. One can see the gazebo is visible in the background.

A view along Rue Pasteur after the fighting.

In this photo one can really see how the Germans transformed the beach into a no man's land covered with larger or smaller points of defence, with an underground network connecting them to each other.

Just after the war, the demolition of the concrete fortifications built between the Observation Post (right) and the port.

Remains of the bunkers in the casino area, with the Observation Post in the background left.

This huge bomb crater attests to the violence
suffered by the bombardment of the city.
Bottom left, the Observation Post intact.

In this photo, taken shortly after the
beginning of the reconstruction work,
we can see that the part of town where
the fighting took place is still virtually
deserted, dominated by the high
silhouette of the Observation Post.

With thanks to the "Grand Bunker"
Museum for the provision of these
photos, constituting the Lesage Fund.

The attack on the casino filmed at Port-en-Bessin

APPENDIX

If the attack on the bunker-casino at Ouistreham was the French Commando's main objective, fifteen years later it would also constitute one of the set pieces of the film *The Longest Day*.

Taken from the eponymous book by historian Cornelius Ryan, this blockbuster by the American producer Darryl Zannuck offered one the greatest displays in the history of cinema, from Robert Mitchum to John Wayne, via Richard Burton, Henry Fonda, Sean Connery, Paul Anka, Clint Eastwood, Curd Jürgens, Arletty, Bourvil and Jean-Louis Barrault. As well as these stars and celebrities, we should add more than twenty thousand extras. To make them feel as much as possible in the skin of the D-Day fighters, the stunt-men learned everything they could from the military, they were taught by a former sergeant in the Wehrmacht who did not hesitate to drag his "recruits" through the mud.

Filming began in spring 1961 in Corsica, when Darryl Zannuck benefitted from the presence of the U.S. 6th Fleet coming to participate in manoeuvres. Shooting followed on the island of Ré, and, of course in Normandy at the Pointe du Hoc, at Caen, on the bridge at Bénouville, in Sainte-Mère-Église... But not at Ouistreham. A new casino was in the course of construction in place of the old one, it was in fact at Port-en-Bessin that the assault against the bunker erected by the Germans (on the foundations of the casino that they had destroyed in 1943) was going

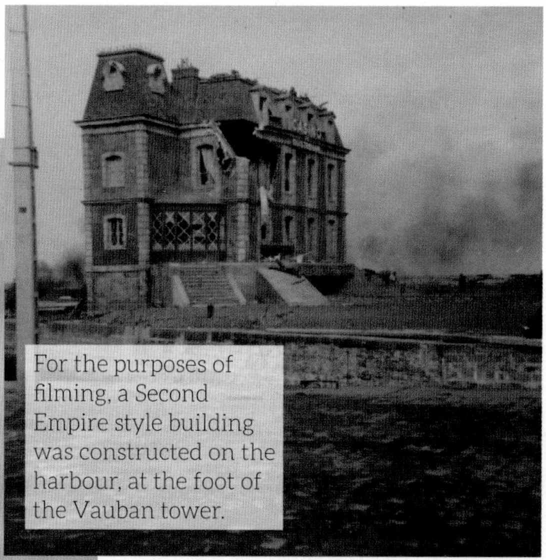

For the purposes of filming, a Second Empire style building was constructed on the harbour, at the foot of the Vauban tower.

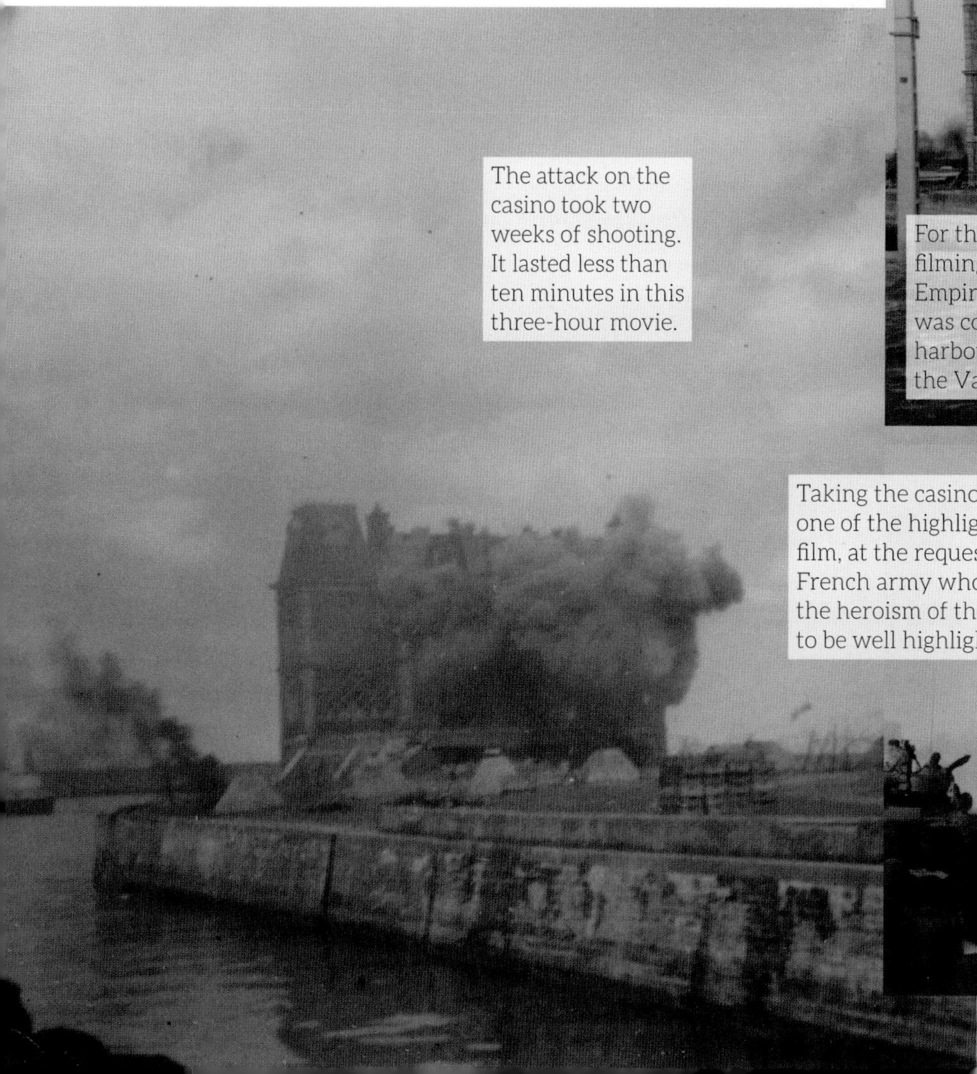

The attack on the casino took two weeks of shooting. It lasted less than ten minutes in this three-hour movie.

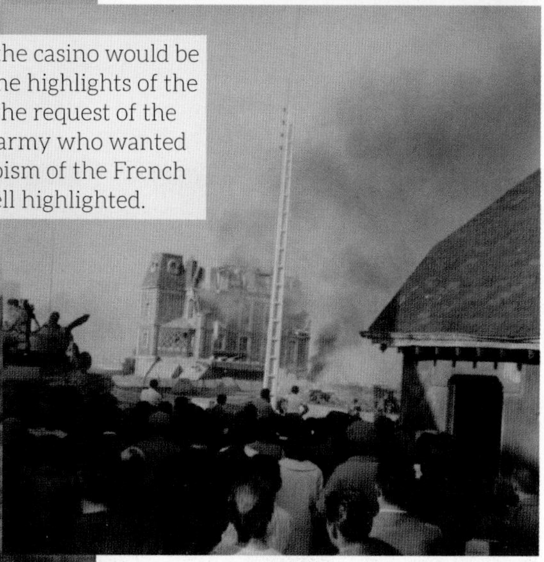

Taking the casino would be one of the highlights of the film, at the request of the French army who wanted the heroism of the French to be well highlighted.

levels, in the style of the Second Empire, curiously built on the port, at the foot of the Vauban tower. Shooting took place between 11 and 29 September 1961 and allowed, in addition to the change of location, a few liberties with the historical reality. Thus, there had never been on June 6 1944, in Ouistreham, nuns who came to treat the wounded soldiers around the casino as there is in the film.

"We must unfortunately acknowledge that the highest flights of fancy presided over the shooting of this part of the film. It is a pity because it would not have been at all difficult to find out about. The only true fact is that the 1st Battalion of marine fusilier commandos landed on June 6 1944, in Riva-Bella. After that there follows a series of departures from the truth." wrote Gwen-Aël Bolloré, one of the nurses of the "177", after attending the screening.

to be reconstructed. For the role of Kieffer, who was present as technical and historical consultant, the production had chosen one of the foremost French actors of the early sixties. Aged 34, as dark and handsome as the real founder of the first *BFMC*, Christian Marquand had begun his screen career in Jean Cocteau's *Beauty and the Beast* in 1946. Ten years later, Roger Vadim propelled him to stardom by casting him opposite Brigitte Bardot in *And God Created Woman*. The objective assigned to the French Green Berets this time however would have nothing to do with the bunker on the Atlantic Wall, quite the opposite. In place of the bunker, the Commandos of the Cross of Lorraine (extras, stunt-men and even authentic Commandos provided by the Navy) attacked another building on three

Despite its flaws, *The Longest Day* is a powerful film and was a great success upon its release in the fall of 1962, attracting a total of nearly 12 million viewers in France alone. Its box office receipts ($25 million the first year on an estimated 8 to 10 million budget) enabled 20th Century Fox to survive the constant budget overruns of other blockbusters made during the same period: Cleopatra with Elizabeth Taylor and Richard Burton, who also fell madly in love during the shooting which could not have been more hectic. Fifteen years after France was liberated, we could say that the Allies had also managed to save the Queen of Egypt. And every time it shows again on TV, the ratings for *The Longest Day* go crazy. Even though the EDF counters no longer jump as they did on its premiere on French television one evening in 1976, when there were so many sets on at the same time the grid could not keep up with it and two regions were brutally deprived of the images: Brittany and Normandy.

This inscription on the wall of the port sector is a testament to the filming; it has been there for more than half a century.

TOUT POUR
LA PECHE
ET LA PLAGE
APPATS. VIVANTS.

Sources & Websites

Interviews with Marcel Riveau, 1986/1987
Interviews with Léon Gautier, 2008/2009
Béret vert, Philipe Kieffer, éditions France-Empire
Commando de la France Libre, Gwen-Aël Bolloré, éditions France Empire
Mille et un jours pour le Jour J, Maurice Chauvet, éditions Michel Lafon
Fusilier marin commando de la France libre, Maurice Chauvet, éditions Italiques
Les Français du Jour J, Georges Fleury, éditions Grasset

Gold, Juno, Sword, Georges Bernage, éditions Heimdal
Sword Beach, Georges Bernage, éditions Heimdal
Ouistreham en guerre, Fabrice Corbin éditions Heimdal
Philippe Kieffer, Benjamin Massieu, éditions Pierre de Taillac
Jour J avec le 1er B.F.M. Commando, éditions Charles Corlet
Aumônier de la France libre, René de Naurois, éditions Grasset
Le commando du 6 juin, Raymond La Sierra, Presses de la Cité

www.ina.fr
www.dday-overlord.com
www.musee-4commando.org
www.defense.gouv.fr/marine

....

Photo Credits

Heimdal Archives, Imperial War Museum, Grand Bunker Museum - Fonds Lesage, Grand Bunker Museum, N°4 Commando Museum, Fabrice Corbin, Erik Groult, Laurent Lemel, Fonds Aubert- Heimdal, Special Collections, ECPAD.

....

With thanks to

Léon Gautier, No.4 Commando Museum (Ouistreham), Gérard Cerizier, Brigitte and Fabrice Corbin, Grand Bunker Museum (Ouistreham), Eric Savigny, the team at Editions Heimdal and especially Erik Groult and Paul Gros for their invaluable assistance all throughout this publishing venture. Not to mention my wife, Laetitia, for her patient and vigilant rereading of the texts.

....

Places to visit

N° 4 Commando Museum
Place Alfred Thomas, 14150 Ouistreham.
Tél : 02 31 96 63 10.

Mémorial Pegasus
Avenue du Major Howard, 14860 Ranville.
Tél : 02.31.78.19.44

The Grand Bunker Museum
Avenue du 6 Juin, 14150 Ouistreham.
Tél : 02 31 97 28 69.

Maquette et infographie : Paul Gros
Mise en page : Erik Groult et Paul Gros

Achevé d'imprimer sur les presses de l'imprimerie Pollina (85407) Luçon, le 15 avril 2014
Georges Bernage, éditeur, © Editions Heimdal 2014
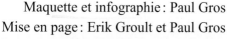

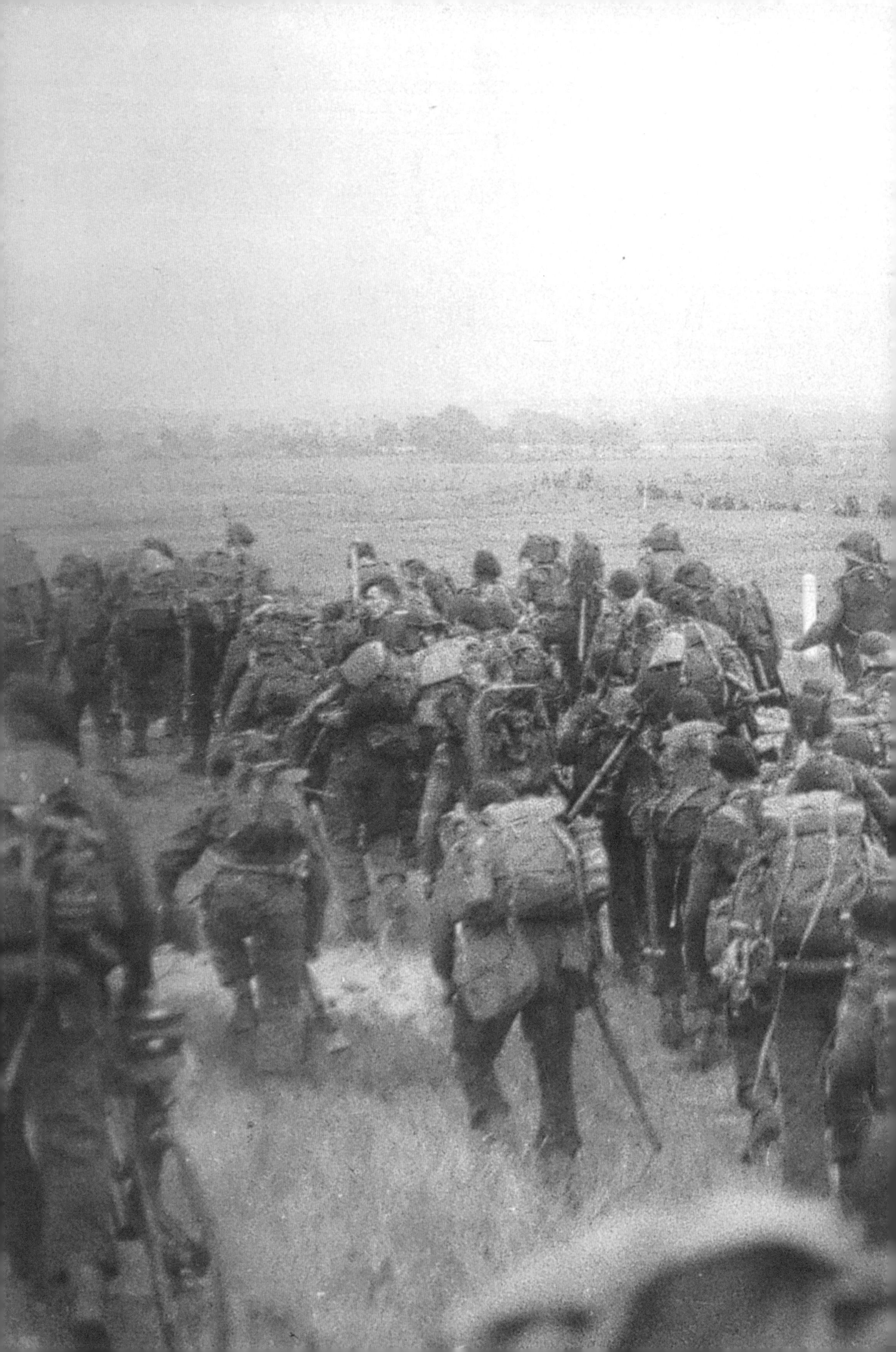